Mutual Savings Banks and
Savings and Loan Associations

Mutual Savings Banks and Savings and Loan Associations: Aspects of Growth

by Alan Teck

Columbia University Press
New York and London
1968

Alan Teck is an economist at
the Federal Reserve Bank of New York.

Copyright © 1967, 1968 Columbia University Press
First published in book form 1968
Library of Congress Catalog Card Number: 68-18999
Printed in the United States of America

To My Parents

Acknowledgments

I OWE A GREAT DEAL to the efforts and patience of Dr. Raymond J. Saulnier, who sponsored this study when it was originally presented as a doctoral dissertation at Columbia University. My gratitude is also extended to Dr. Roger Murray and other members of the Columbia University faculty who made many helpful suggestions.

In addition, I have had the good fortune to interview many people in the mutual savings bank and savings and loan association industries, and I would particularly like to acknowledge the assistance and encouragement given by Leon Kendall, Saul Klaman, David Fritz, and Gerald Seixas.

Although this study is my independent work and the views expressed in it are mine and not to be attributed in any sense to others, I wish gratefully to acknowledge financial aid received during the period of its conduct through a Columbia University President's Fellowship and a grant from the Mutual Savings Foundation of America. Also without assuming responsibility for any of the materials or conclusions of the study, my employer, the Federal Reserve Bank of New York, freed some of my time for work on the project and permitted Philip Krackow to prepare the charts. My wife Kathy provided important editorial and proofreading assistance.

ALAN TECK

New York
October, 1967

Contents

Tables

Charts

Mutual Savings Banks and Savings and Loan Associations

Introduction

IN THEIR FORMATIVE YEARS, savings and loan associations and mutual savings banks used different methods to provide different financial services for people trying to solve different economic problems. In recent decades both types of institutions have been using similar methods to provide almost identical services for people with essentially the same economic objectives. Despite this functional convergence, and also despite a substantial structural convergence, the savings and loan industry has been growing more rapidly than the mutual savings bank industry since the mid-1930s, not only in the United States as a whole but also in every state in which both types of institutions are located. This book examines the period 1945 through 1964 in an attempt to explain this apparent contradiction.

The analysis leads to the conclusion that individuals with accounts either in savings and loan associations or mutual savings banks demonstrated an overwhelming preference for doing business with organizations located close to their homes, jobs, or shopping districts. Simple regression analysis indicates a direct and highly significant relationship between local changes in total personal income and in the growth of individual institutions. Thus, an underlying reason for the persistent differences in growth is that mutual savings banks, owing to their earlier development and to restrictive legislation affecting branches, have been heavily concentrated in large urban centers where population has been declining and where average per capita income has been rising less rapidly than in most suburban and other nonurban regions. Savings and loan associations, on the other hand, having mostly developed later and having been favored by more liberal branching privileges, are more widely dispersed not only throughout the nation but also in suburban areas and other neighborhoods of more rapid population growth. The importance of the location factor is underscored by the fact that savings and loan associations have achieved their higher growth rates even in many regions where mutual savings banks have offered higher average interest payments for many years and where both types of institutions have appeared to be offering similar safety and liquidity for their deposit and savings accounts.

While interest payment spreads between savings and loan associations and mutual savings banks were a comparatively unimportant factor influencing their relative growth rates from 1945 through 1964, interest payment competition from commercial banks, government securities, and other savings media was significantly more important. The analysis suggests that a partial explanation for the fact that differences between the average growth rates of savings and loan associations and mutual savings banks widened from 1945 through the mid-1950s and narrowed thereafter is that it was not until the mid-1950s that interest payment spreads between savings and loan associations and commercial banks declined to the point where the growth of the former was significantly affected. The growth of mutual savings banks, on the other hand, was affected by commercial bank competition during the entire period, as their location forced them to compete more directly with the largest and most aggressive commercial banks. In addition, and also because of their location, mutual savings banks have been more directly affected than savings and loan associations by competition from investment opportunities offered by government and private securities.

Currently, growth differentials among thrift institutions are undergoing change. In 1966 the rate of net savings growth in mutual savings banks as a group exceeded that in savings and loan associations for the first time since the early 1930s, while in 1967 the more typical relationship was restored. Nevertheless —and regardless of which type of institution grows more rapidly —these movements do not change the basic fact, demonstrated by the 1945–64 data, that mutual savings banks must offset the disadvantages of their present locations if they are to compete with the more widely dispersed savings and loan associations.

Based on this analysis and on the principle of providing similar opportunities for institutions offering substantially similar services, this book argues that mutual savings banks should be given greater opportunities for moving out of large urban centers into rapidly growing communities by granting them broader branching possibilities and a dual chartering system similar to those currently available to the savings and loan association industry. Moreover, it is argued that mutual savings banks should be permitted to increase the range of savings services that they could profitably and safely offer from their present locations. If legislative restrictions continue to keep these institutions from expanding geographically and from developing new services, the ability of mutual savings banks to respond safely and competitively to current and future savings needs will be seriously impaired.

1
Early History

MUTUAL SAVINGS BANKS

THE FIRST MUTUAL SAVINGS BANKS were organized exclusively with the needs of the saver in mind: their purpose was to encourage thrift among people of modest means by providing facilities where comparatively small savings could be deposited safely and with profit. The earliest organizations formed specifically to provide services similar to those supplied by mutual savings banks in the United States today were started in England and Scotland. Their development into nationwide industries followed a pattern frequently noted by historians of institutional change: [1] first, changing social conditions create new needs; second, there is an attempt to satisfy these needs with existing institutions; third, available institutions being unable to do the job adequately, dissatisfaction mounts; finally new ideas are conceived, some are tried, and those that are successful are developed into new institutions.

BEGINNINGS IN ENGLAND AND SCOTLAND

In Britain, the industrial revolution produced changes that called for new financial services. These changes included the development of conditions typically associated with the emergence of a factory system and the payment of money wages.

[1] For example, see Neil J. Smelser, *Social Change in the Industrial Revolution* (Chicago: University of Chicago Press, 1959), chapter 1.

Many people began almost immediately to enjoy the higher standards of living generated by industrialization, and along with this went important changes in living habits and in patterns of consumption and saving. Many workingmen, for example, felt the need for a place in which to store funds not immediately necessary for the purchase of goods and services—a place where savings would be safe and liquid and, hopefully, where they would earn interest. At the same time, the rapid movement of people from farms to areas surrounding newly opened mines and factories created noticeable increases in unemployment. Many families previously relying on farming or on association with a farming community for their daily needs now found themselves with neither funds nor land nor benefactors. An awareness of this situation, as well as of the wage earners' desire for savings deposit facilities, induced many people to experiment, both in theory and in practice, with ideas that were ultimately to lead to the first mutual savings bank.

Long before the earliest such banks were started, other institutions had been formed to meet the need for organized thrift facilities. The craft guilds of the Middle Ages, for example, developed charitable funds to which members contributed for their own relief in time of sickness, unemployment, and old age and for the assistance of their widows and children. But craft guilds never served unorganized workers, and perhaps even more to the point, their importance decreased rapidly as they proved unadaptable to the new conditions of industrial life. By the latter part of the eighteenth century, a large and rapidly increasing number of wage earners found themselves without organized facilities for depositing savings or for establishing independent funds for their personal security.

For most people, churches were the principal relief agencies, although from time to time programs to aid the poor were provided by the state as well. But as problems of unemployment and vagrancy became more pronounced, the doctrine of self-help began to be advocated with increasing frequency. One of the most vigorous exponents of the self-help approach—a person sometimes referred to as the originator of the mutual savings banking idea—was the author Daniel Defoe. As early as 1698, in his "Essay on Projects," Defoe suggested a plan by which all the workmen of a community would pay a portion of their wages into a central fund. The accumulated money was to be invested; savers were to receive a modest return on their principal; the remaining interest would be given to the poor. Over the next hundred years, similar ideas were expounded by some of the most noted economists and social critics of the day.[2] In 1797, for instance, Jeremy Bentham proposed a plan that he called a "frugality bank." Under it, people with modest incomes would save systematically and be rewarded with interest earned by investing the collected funds.[3]

Ideas similar to those of Defoe and Bentham found their way into practice, and by the turn of the eighteenth century, projects called Christmas banks, penny banks, and Sunday banks were fairly common in England.[4] In Christmas banks (usually located in the home of a responsible individual), money was deposited regularly and returned in a lump sum at the beginning of December. No interest was paid; the idea was that having money for Christmas was a sufficient reward for systematic saving. In penny banks, people typically deposited a few pennies each week and received a dividend every few months. If their savings had not been regular, they usually forfeited the dividends. Sunday banks, as their name implies, were operated only on Sunday by people who pursued other interests during the week. In the case of penny banks and Sunday banks, the accumulated funds were typically placed with commercial banks that accepted the accounts as a favor to the organizing philanthropists. In the earliest groups, it was not uncommon for

[2] The plans of Defoe, Bentham, Adam Smith, Ricardo, Malthus, and others are discussed in Oliver Horne, *A History of Savings Banks* (London: Oxford University Press, 1947), chapters 1–3.

[3] The novelty of this and similar ideas can be fully appreciated only in their proper historical context. During this period, most people had no place to save money other than in their own homes; for private individuals to store funds in some central place and receive interest payments on very small savings balances was a revolutionary thought.

[4] On early British savings banks, see William Lewins, *A History of Banks for Savings* (London: Sampson, Low, Son, and Marston, 1886), chapters 2–3; also Horne, chapters 1–3.

the founder to pay the interest or dividends out of his own pocket.[5]

The Tottenham and Ruthwell Banks

Among the various savings services being offered, probably the first to be tried on a large enough scale to be considered a close forerunner of the modern mutual savings bank was the Tottenham Benefit Bank started in 1804 by Priscilla Wakefield. After many years of experience with a wide range of philanthropic organizations (including a Female Benefit Fund and a Children's Bank), Mrs. Wakefield decided that a thrift experiment based on the concept of self-help was worth trying on a wide scale. Reflecting on her thoughts, she wrote:

From observing that many of the poor, particularly servants, either squandered away their savings or lent them to those less prudent than themselves, from the want of a convenient opportunity of placing them where they would be secure, it occurred to me that an association might be formed which would afford them complete safety, in their own neighborhood, by the guarantee of a few respectable persons or property.[6]

Once organized, the Tottenham Benefit Bank was opened on the first Monday of each month to receive (and to repay upon demand) any sum from a shilling upwards. Interest of 5 per

[5] Most early savings plans were strongly influenced by three developments. The first was the widely held belief that an individual could best advance his personal welfare, and that of the nation generally, by acting in his own self-interest, expecting no help from the church, state, or any philanthropic group. Reflecting this "laissez-faire" attitude, most savings projects emphasized the importance of self-help and independently established personal security. The second was the breakdown of the medieval Catholic attitude that considered worldly activity a form of vanity and the emergence of Protestant sects which approved of secular endeavor as an index of spiritual worth. The third was knowledge about banks in such cities as Hamburg, Göttingen, Zurich, and Bern that were accepting small deposits from working people, investing them profitably, and paying dividends to their savers. Banks on the continent, however, were less like modern mutual savings banks than those started subsequently in Scotland and England. For example, they usually accepted money only when it was to be used for a predefined purpose, and they rarely allowed withdrawals at the discretion of the savers. But their success with small accounts drew considerable attention and created a favorable impression. For a history of early European banks, see Henry W. Wolff, *Peoples Banks* (London: P. S. King, 1919).

[6] Horne, pp. 25–26.

cent each year was allowed on every complete pound. At first,
all deposited funds were placed in a commercial bank, but after
a time most of them were used to purchase Government "five
per cents." Benevolent guarantors made up the difference
whenever the income was insufficient to pay the necessary dividends. Thus, on the basis of this comparatively simple organization, Mrs. Wakefield can fairly be regarded as the practical originator of the first mutual savings bank.

However, when one thinks of individuals who were most influential in spreading the concept of mutual savings banking,
attention invariably turns to the Reverend Henry Duncan
—the man usually called the "father of mutual savings banking." Duncan organized a mutual savings bank in Ruthwell,
Scotland, in 1810, and after its formation he met with substantial success in his efforts to encourage leaders in other communities to follow his example.[7] Furthermore, believing that mutual
savings banking would ultimately become a large industry of
great public value, he spent considerable effort working for a
law that would allow these institutions the same tax exemptions
then being granted friendly societies. Even though taxes were
comparatively light, once the law was passed there was a sharp
increase in the number of mutual savings banks in Scotland and
subsequently in England.

The principle behind the Ruthwell bank was the same as that
underlying the Tottenham Benefit Bank and essentially similar
to that behind all mutual savings banking today. It was designed to encourage frugality through the provision of services
by which people of modest incomes could help themselves by
storing funds safely and with profit. The major differences between the Ruthwell organization and the mutual savings banks
of today appear on the investment side of the balance sheet.
The Ruthwell group, like the Tottenham Bank before it, deposited all of its money in a commercial bank, while today, of
course, the investments of mutual savings banks are consider-

---

[7] For a description of Duncan's bank and of his efforts on behalf of mutual
savings banking, see Lewins, pp. 27–44, and Franklin J. Sherman, *Modern Story of
Mutual Savings Banks* (New York: Little and Ives, 1934), pp. 23–29.

ably more diversified. Unlike the Tottenham Bank, however, the later organization declared dividends only from its earnings, without relying on the contributions of benefactors. The Ruthwell bank was an immediate success and its rapid growth attracted widespread attention. As one historian notes: "By the end of 1815 Scotland was well covered with newly formed savings banks." [8]

News of this rapidly expanding industry quickly spread to England, where previously mentioned efforts—penny banks, Sunday banks, and Christmas banks, as well as the Tottenham Benefit Bank—had already created a familiarity with the mutual savings bank approach. By 1819, when the first three mutual savings banks were organized in the United States, well over three hundred such banks were operating in almost all parts of England, Wales, and Ireland.

DEVELOPMENT IN THE UNITED STATES

During the forty-one years from the end of the Revolutionary War to the organization of the first mutual savings bank in the United States in 1819, there were many social changes similar to those experienced in eighteenth-century England. Population grew rapidly as immigration and birth rates rose sharply; a factory system began to develop; transition from barter to a money economy was largely accomplished. These conditions in turn created financial problems similar in many respects to those in England.

Expanding industrial and commercial activities, for example, produced an ever-increasing number of wage earners who were faced with the problem of finding a place to store savings. Hiding money at home was unsafe and unprofitable; commercial banks, the only type of private institution accepting deposits during that period, did not welcome small individual accounts; no government agency provided savings deposit facilities; and government securities were in denominations beyond the means

[8] Horne, p. 52.

of the average wage earner. At the same time, although the nation as a whole was faced with a shortage of labor, in some regions there was difficulty providing stable, year-round employment for all who came seeking factory work. And as in England, once workers were without farms or other means of support, the severity of difficulties associated with unemployment increased.

Faced with the desirability of providing wage earners with a safe and profitable place to store savings, and at the same time hoping to ameliorate at least a few of the problems of unemployment, some citizens turned to the idea of developing mutual thrift institutions. In at least a few cases, familiarity with cooperative organizations and a knowledge of mutual savings banking in England combined to suggest that institutions of this type might be profitably formed in the United States. As in England, it was hoped that, by encouraging thrift among working people, financial self-reliance would be promoted and some aspects of poverty prevented.[9]

The Bank for Savings in the City of New York

Records indicate that Thomas Eddy and DeWitt Clinton of New York, James Savage of Boston, and Condy Raguet of Philadelphia all received correspondence in 1815 and 1816 concerning the organization of mutual savings banks in England and that subsequently each of these men was influential in the formation of a mutual savings bank in his home town.[10] Credit for being the first group to receive a state charter goes to the Boston organization;[11] but records show that the Philadelphia Savings Fund Society had previously started accepting savings, although

[9] For a discussion of these developments, see Emerson W. Keyes, *A History of Savings Banking in the United States, 1816–1877* (New York: Bradford Rhodes, 1878), Vol. I, chapter 1.

[10] See Sherman, pp. 35–55.

[11] Notification that the charter had been granted appeared in the *Christian Disciples*, a leading Boston newspaper of that day. It makes the English origin of the bank quite clear by reporting that the Provident Institution for Savings "proposed to form an institution in Boston for the security and improvement of the savings of persons of humble life . . . similar [to] institutions exist[ing] in England and Scotland." Quoted in John Lintner, *Mutual Savings Banks in the Savings and Mortgage Markets* (Boston: Harvard University, Graduate School of Business Administration, 1948), pp. 46–47.

without state authorization. Going back even one step farther, the first group to keep minutes of discussions that were to lead ultimately to the formation of a mutual savings bank was comprised of the men who started The Bank for Savings in the City of New York. Inasmuch as there is more evidence available about this institution than about either of its predecessors, its early development is discussed below.

The purpose for which The Bank for Savings was started was essentially the same as that for which all preceding mutual savings banks in England and Scotland had been organized and fundamentally similar to the underlying purpose of all succeeding mutual savings banks in the United States. It was to accept deposits and to allow withdrawals in amounts and at times to be decided on by the savers, to invest these funds safely, and to use the profits for expenses, additions to reserves, and dividend payments to depositors. In the words of the Act of Incorporation, the Bank was to afford "the two-fold advantage of security and interest," and this in turn was considered "a laudable attempt to ameliorate the condition of the poor and labouring class of the community." [12]

In accordance with its basic purpose, The Bank for Savings gave special attention to the accounts of people in lower income groups.[13] As stated in the Act of Incorporation, the organization was to accept "such small sums of money as may be saved from the earnings of Tradesmen, Mechanics, Labourers, Minors, Servants, and others." [14]

[12] The entire Act of Incorporation, as well as the best early history of The Bank for Savings in the City of New York, appears in Charles E. Knowles, *History of The Bank for Savings in the City of New York, 1819–1929* (New York: The Bank for Savings in the City of New York, 1929).

[13] Today, in addition to individual deposits, mutual savings banks may hold accounts of philanthropic, educational, and other nonprofit organizations; corporate accounts are prohibited. In some states there is a limit on the amount that can be held in each type of deposit.

[14] The object of serving the needs of people of modest means was well achieved in practice. As The Bank for Savings' first annual report indicates, of the 1,527 depositors at the end of the first year, the largest occupational category was domestic servants (143), followed by clerks (65), cooks (35), seamstresses (34), and so on, with only a handful of merchants and professional men. Of the 2,443 deposit accounts opened during the first year, 821 were under $5, over half were under $10, and approximately 85 per cent were under $50. Knowles, pp. 164, 172–73.

Among the other characteristics common to The Bank for Savings and all subsequent mutual savings banks in the United States were the right to a perpetual existence, the trustee system, the method of management, and the claim to mutuality.

The right to a perpetual existence was the most difficult provision to obtain from the chartering legislature. During this period, all commercial banks, and the First and Second Banks of the United States as well, were being granted terminating charters, and needless to say, legislators were reluctant to give up the control over banking institutions implied by the ability to deny charter renewal applications. But the Bank's advocates refused to back down on this point, although they were flexible about the manner in which it was achieved. When the Act of Incorporation was finally granted, in 1819, the board of trustees (rather than the Bank itself) was given the right to "perpetual succession." This in effect gave the Bank the right to a continuing existence.

A second structural aspect that The Bank for Savings copied directly from its English predecessors was the trustee system. Under the Act of Incorporation, the twenty-eight men who had been active in the Bank's formation became its first trustees (or directors, as they were then called). These trustees were given the responsibility for overseeing all of the organization's activities, and an indication of the motives and attitudes with which these men accepted their position is reflected in the words of William Bayard, the first president of the Bank. He observed: "The directors [trustees] owe it both to the public and themselves distinctly to declare that they entirely disclaim the idea of receiving any personal emolument or advantage in any shape whatever." [15] This concept was translated into a strict requirement when the Act of Incorporation explicitly stated that trustees should "not directly or indirectly receive any pay or emolument for their services, not transact any business which belongs to or is transacted by [The Bank for Savings]." [16]

[15] Knowles, p. 41.
[16] *Ibid.*, p. 164.

With respect to depositors, mutual savings bank trustees occupy a strictly fiduciary position, and, over the years, prohibitions against self-dealing and profiting collaterally from the activities of the institutions have been broadly interpreted and strictly applied. The absence of a personal profit motive among trustees has been one of the fundamental concepts of mutual savings banking down to the present.

During the early months of its existence, the trustees of The Bank for Savings elected officers from among their own number, performed the bookkeeping, and jointly formed the "attending committees" that handled the daily transactions. As the Bank grew, however, full-time personnel were hired and the trustees' role became more and more supervisory. In less than ten years, the managerial functions had been turned over entirely to trustee-appointed, salaried officers.

Another aspect of The Bank for Savings that appears in the structure of all subsequent mutual savings banks pertains to membership and mutuality. The Bank had no members. It had only trustees, officers, a staff, and depositors; unlike commercial banks, it had no stockholders. Depositors were creditors of the organization, and nothing more. With one exception, they had none of the rights or obligations typically associated with the concepts of membership or ownership. Depositors did not, for example, vote for either trustees or management; they did not attend meetings; they had no authority or obligations for decision making of any operational significance. Furthermore, they had no influence over the way the Bank invested their money, handled their accounts, or paid interest.

In an operating mutual savings bank there is nothing stated or implied indicating that either the term "member" or "owner" is or should be applicable to depositors in any structural or functional sense. The term "mutual" only indicates that all distributed earnings must be shared by the depositors. The only ownership claim that mutual savings bank depositors have becomes effective when their organizations are liquidated. At that time the current depositors are entitled to receive distribution of the surplus (net assets less all debts and deposits) according to the proportion which their respective deposits bear to the aggregate balance of all deposits.[17]

Based on concepts of perpetual existence, a trustee system, and profit-sharing among depositors, The Bank for Savings in the City of New York began operations in 1819, and judging by its deposit growth, it began immediately to fill an important need in this city of almost a quarter of a million people. At the end of its first day of operations, eighty people had deposited $2,807; by the close of the first month, this amount had risen to over $40,000. When the Bank issued its first six-month report, the figure had increased to $153,378 and there were 1,527 deposit accounts.[18]

By September, 1963, The Bank for Savings in The City of New York had assets of almost three quarters of a billion dollars. During that month it was merged with the New York Savings Bank and became The New York Bank for Savings. Today the combined institution has assets of over one and a half billion dollars.

Other Early Mutual Savings Banks in the United States

Between the inception and the chartering of The Bank for Savings, two other mutual savings banks were opened—the Provident Institution for Savings in Boston and the Philadelphia Savings Fund Society. In 1819, two more were started—one in Baltimore and a second in Salem, Massachusetts. These five institutions were eminently successful, and news of their operations spread quickly. In 1820, five more were organized, and these also grew rapidly. Today, each of the first ten mutual savings banks is a leading savings institution in its home city.

Table 1 indicates that, in terms of the number of institutions, the industry's growth was concentrated in the nineteenth century. Thereafter, the number of mutual savings banks started

[17] Legal precedents that discuss depositors' rights to the distribution of surplus include *In re: The Dissolution of Cleveland Savings Society*, Ohio Ct. Com. Pls. (1961); *Morristown Institution for Savings* v. *Roberts, et al.*, 42 N.J. Eq. 496, 8 Atl. 315 (1887).
[18] Knowles, pp. 172–73.

TABLE 1

Mutual Savings Banks in the United States, 1820–1964

Year	Number of Banks	Total Deposits (in millions)	Number of Deposit Accounts (in thousands)	Average Deposit
1820	10	$ 1	8	$ 132
1830	36	2	16	150
1840	61	14	78	179
1850	108	43	251	173
1860	278	149	693	215
1870	517	549	1,630	337
1880	629	819	2,336	351
1890	637	1,336	3,765	325
1900	652	2,134	5,370	397
1910	638	3,361	7,480	449
1920	620	5,172	9,445	547
1930	606	9,191	11,895	772
1940	540	10,618	15,624	680
1950	529	20,025	19,264	1,040
1960	515	36,343	22,493	1,616
1964	506	48,849	22,231	2,197

Sources: Data through 1940 from John Lintner, *Mutual Savings Banks in the Savings and Mortgage Markets* (Boston: Harvard University, Graduate School of Business Administration, 1948), p. 49; subsequent years from National Association of Mutual Savings Banks, *National Fact Book* (New York: National Association of Mutual Savings Banks, 1965), pp. 8, 10.

to decline. With respect to deposits and the number of deposit accounts, expansion was rapid in the early decades: by 1830, 16,000 depositors held approximately two million dollars in 36 mutual savings banks. By the turn of the century, there were 652 banks with an estimated $2.1 billion in over five million deposit accounts.

The rapid growth of mutual savings banks in the United States during the nineteenth century largely reflects the fact that they were performing services for which there was considerable demand and no close substitutes. Among the financial organizations that would subsequently provide similar services, commercial banks were still reluctant to accept small deposits and savings and loan associations were concerned almost exclusively with financing the construction and purchase of homes.

But regardless of the rapidity of their growth in the East, mutual savings banks generally failed to move into the South or the West. Even today, as Table 2 indicates, almost all mutual

TABLE 2

Number of Mutual Savings Banks, December 31, 1964, by State and Period of Organization

	Total	Prior to 1849	1850 to 1899	1900 to 1939	1939 to 1964
New York	125	17	95	13	
Massachusetts	179	38	132	8	1
Connecticut	71	11	57	3	
Pennsylvania	7	2	5		
New Jersey	21	2	19		
Maryland	6	2	4		
New Hampshire	32	6	23	3	
Rhode Island	7	4	3		
Maine	32	3	28	1	
Washington	4		1	1	2
Minnesota	1		1		
Delaware	2	1	1		
Vermont	6	1	5		
Indiana	4		4		
Oregon	1			1	
Ohio	2		2		
Wisconsin	4		1	3	
Alaska	1				1
Virgin Islands	1				1
Total	506	87	381	33	5

Sources: National Association of Mutual Savings Banks, *Mutual Savings Banking: Basic Characteristics and Role in the National Economy* (Englewood Cliffs, N.J.: Prentice-Hall, 1962), p. 31; recent data received directly from the National Association of Mutual Savings Banks.

savings banks are in eleven northeastern states. In the nineteenth and the early twentieth century, the lack of geographic diversity in the spread of mutual savings banks was primarily the result of economic conditions, but in recent decades legal limitations have also been important restrictive factors. Throughout the earlier period, the major occupations in the South and the West were agriculture and, to a lesser extent, mining and lumbering. Unlike the manufacturing and commercial centers of the northeast, these regions did not have large numbers of wage earners, and there was very little demand for places to store savings. On the contrary, a shortage of capital existed, and the primary financial need was for institutions to supply credit. Thus, as might be expected, commercial banks moved into these areas, and by the time industrial activity produced a large number of wage earners with funds to save, these organizations were in a position to add savings services to the range of facilities already being offered. Perhaps more to the point, once commercial banks began accepting small individual savings accounts, they eliminated the need that had previously motivated philanthropic-minded citizens to start mutual savings banks.

A second requirement typically found in newly settled areas was for financing to facilitate the construction and purchase of homes, and the earliest building and loan associations were organized specifically to satisfy this need. These organizations, like commercial banks, spread throughout the South and West, and it was a comparatively simple process for them to adapt their services to accommodate local demands for deposit facilities as such needs developed. By the turn of the twentieth century, many building and loan associations were accepting savings deposits in a manner essentially the same as that used by mutual savings banks in the northeast.

Thus, with both building and loan associations and commercial banks providing thrift services throughout most of the southern and western states, incentives to organize mutual savings banks were largely eliminated. Today, however, the geographic concentration of the mutual savings bank industry, originally the result almost exclusively of economic forces, is enforced by legislation that allows mutual savings banks to be chartered only in the eighteen states in which they currently operate. Savings and loan associations, on the other hand, may be chartered in any state of the nation.

SAVINGS AND LOAN ASSOCIATIONS [19]

Savings and loan associations in the United States are descended directly from English building societies, which, like the earliest mutual savings banks, were a product of England's industrial revolution. Throughout most of the eighteenth century, the mass migration from farms to newly opened mines and factories, the sharp advance in immigration from Ireland and Scotland, and rising birth rates in combination with declining mortality rates greatly increased the demand for housing, especially in some of England's most rapidly growing industrial centers. At the same time, the emergence of a factory system brought higher living standards to many people, extended the practice of paying money wages, and created jobs that frequently required the full-time energies of entire families. It was not long, therefore, before it became clear to many people that it would be practical to have a mechanism through which part of their wages could be used to finance the purchase or construction of homes.

In a few situations, employers built living accommodations in an attempt to attract and hold a labor force, but these were typically dormitory residences not well suited to the needs of family life. As to other alternatives, it quickly became apparent that neither commercial banks nor any government agency would make small loans to finance home construction. Thus, the basic problem persisted and some people with steady incomes and the ability to save began to consider the possibility of financing their homes through some form of cooperative self-help. One of these efforts, by a group in the factory town of

[19] The term "savings and loan association" was not widely used in the United States until the 1930s. Prior to that, names such as "building society," "building and loan association," "homestead association," and "cooperative bank" were more common. When this study refers to events in the United States prior to the 1930s, the term "building and loan association" is used; when subsequent events are discussed, the term "savings and loan association" is applied.

Birmingham, England, led to the formation, in 1781, of the first building society on record.[20]

The Birmingham Building Society

As has been the case with many British institutions, the Birmingham Building Society was organized in a pub, and it was in this congenial atmosphere that its monthly meetings were held. The structure of the organization was simple. Its founders were its owners and sole participants. They were mutually responsible for its activities, and they alone shared in its benefits. There were no arrangements for accepting savings from people who did not want financing for a home, and there were no provisions for making loans to nonmembers. Each year the participants elected officers from among their own number, and these "proprietors" (the equivalent of today's directors) served the group's interests and supervised its activities without pay.

The procedures of the Birmingham Building Society can be determined from the eight articles under which it was organized.[21] In brief, they indicate that each member was to come to the "Fountain" in Cheapside sometime during the evening of the first Monday of every month and give the treasurer half a guinea for each share to which he had subscribed. If a member did not show up, he was fined; if he failed to make payments for an extended period, he was liable to forfeit what he had previously paid into the treasury.

[20] Home financing organizations are reported to have existed in ancient Egypt, China, and the South Sea Islands, but records of the structure and operations of these groups are unavailable. It is clear, however, that these institutions had no direct influence on the building and loan associations organized in the United States. For a discussion of the earlier organizations, see Horace F. Clark and Frank A. Chase, *Elements of the Modern Building and Loan Association* (New York: The Macmillan Company, 1925), pp. 452-56. For details on the Birmingham Building Society, see John A. Langford, *A Century of Birmingham Life; or, A Chronicle of Local Events, 1741–1841* (Birmingham: E. C. Osborne, 1868).

[21] The "Articles" of the Birmingham Building Society appear in their entirety in Harold Bellman, *The Building Society Movement* (London: Methuen and Co., 1927), pp. 5–6. Additional information is in J. B. Leaver, "The Historical and Legal Development of British Building Societies," *Yearbook of the United States Building and Loan League, 1894* (Chicago: United States Building and Loan League, 1895), pp. 142–55.

When the fund had increased sufficiently, lots were drawn to see who would get the first loan. The winner was entitled to £70 for each of his shares. After receiving the loan, he selected a building site on land leased by the organization, submitted construction plans to an inspection committee, and began building when the plans were approved.

When his house was completed, the owner began monthly repayments on the principal of his loan; he also started paying 5 per cent interest on its face value, and continued making the regular monthly payments on his shares. Security was required for the loan, but a mortgage on the house itself was acceptable. Each time sufficient funds were accumulated, a new loan was made and a new house started. After every member had received and repaid a loan, the remaining fund was divided among the members and the Birmingham Building Society was terminated.

This method of turning savings into investments in housing seemed to work well, and the idea spread. By 1783, two similar groups had been organized in London and another in Birmingham.[22] Yet, for at least two reasons, the building society movement did not develop as rapidly as did the subsequent mutual savings bank movement.

First, a building society was a more complicated organization. Whereas a mutual savings bank depositor was a creditor who could deposit and withdraw any amount of money at any time, the member of a building society was a part owner who had to make rather sizable monthly payments on his shares as well as systematic repayments on his loan. Moreover, he had to be capable of performing managerial functions if elected to office and be qualified to assume the liabilities of joint ownership. This meant that the building society member had to be assured of a steady job, with an income large enough to allow substantial savings to be set aside on a contractual basis. Thus, membership in a building society was limited to a much smaller

22 For figures on the spread of building societies in eighteenth- and nineteenth-century England, see Henry W. Brabook, "Statistics of Building Societies," *Yearbook of the United States Building and Loan League, 1930* (Chicago: United States Building and Loan League, 1931), pp. 19–31.

group than were the deposit services of a mutual savings bank.

A second factor retarding the spread of building societies was that not until 1836 (fifty-five years after the formation of the Birmingham Building Society) did Parliament pass an act differentiating building societies from friendly societies, explicitly granting both types of institutions complete exemption from all income and property taxes. At end of 1836, there were an estimated 491 building societies in England and Wales with approximately 273,593 members and annual receipts of £13,000,000.[23] All of these figures began to rise rapidly immediately after the Act was passed, and in 1850 there were over 2,000 building societies registered throughout England. By that time the movement had also spread to all parts of the Commonwealth and into many sections of the United States as well.[24]

BEGINNINGS IN THE UNITED STATES

The first building and loan associations in the United States were organized with the hope that they would help solve home financing problems similar to those in eighteenth- and nineteenth-century England. During the fifty years from the Revolutionary War to the formation of the first building and loan association, the population of the United States rose fourfold. As a result, there was a sharp increase in the need for housing, especially in major industrial and commercial communities. Concurrently, the factory system was bringing higher living standards to an increasing number of people and expanding the use of money wages. As towns and cities grew and materials became scarcer, wage earners frequently lacked the time or inclination to build their own homes, and people were increasingly in a position to buy a home. But it was typically necessary either to obtain credit to make the acquisition or to develop a method for accumulating savings in advance of purchase.

[23] *Ibid.*, p. 28.
[24] For an account of the spread of the building society movement through England, Wales, and the Commonwealth, see Bellman.

Confronted with this situation, and in the absence of institutions willing to make home financing loans, the logical move was from individual to group action. English settlers familiar with the British building societies used their knowledge of those organizations to set up almost identical operations in the United States.

The Oxford Provident

The first building and loan association in the United States was organized in 1831 in the small factory town of Frankford, Pennsylvania.[25] As new settlers arrived to work in the textile and tanning mills, they needed housing. And as most of them soon became wage earners, it was not long before they sought to develop an efficient way to turn savings into home financing. Most of these early settlers had originally come from England (Frankford had previously been called Oxford), and many were undoubtedly familiar with the building societies then operating throughout the British Isles. It was a natural step, therefore, when two factory owners and a doctor, all from England, proposed that a building society be formed. The response was immediate, and the first Oxford Provident was started less than a year after the proposal.

Its constitution stated that the Oxford Provident was a specialized organization formed solely "to enable contributors thereof to build or purchase dwelling houses." [26] After this had been accomplished, the remaining fund was to be divided among the members and the association terminated.

The corporate body of the Oxford Provident, like that of its English predecessors, was composed of members who mutually shared the ownership and management of the association. Each member was required to attend monthly meetings (or incur a

25 The following paragraphs rely heavily on information in Morton Bodfish and A. D. Theobald, *Savings and Loan Principles* (Englewood Cliffs, N.J.: Prentice-Hall, 1940), pp. 30–39, and Morton Bodfish, ed., *History of Building and Loan in the United States* (Chicago: United States Building and Loan League, 1931), pp. 32–34.

26 The entire constitution of the Oxford Provident appears in Bodfish, *History*, pp. 37–42.

fine), and he was to participate in the decisions of the association through discussions, by voting on a wide range of issues, and by helping to elect the board of trustees. The thirty-six charter members reserved the right to refuse admittance to anyone applying for shares subsequent to the organization's formation, while at the same time they gave themselves the right to withdraw from the group with one month's notice.

The Oxford Provident was managed by thirteen trustees (called directors in modern savings and loan associations) elected from among the members to serve one-year terms. These trustees supervised all operations; their jobs ranged from giving financial advice to members, to setting up committees for appraising property, examining land and titles, holding deeds, checking on construction specifications and insurance provisions, etc. For these activities, the trustees did not receive "either directly or indirectly any compensation for their services." [27]

The operations of the Oxford Provident were basically the same as those of the Birmingham Building Society. Its funds came solely from membership "dues," consisting of an initiation fee of $5.00 per share and monthly payments of $3.00 on each share. Fines of 25¢ were imposed if payments were delinquent; if a person fell an entire year in arrears, he was automatically expelled.

Because each member was ultimately to receive a loan, there were no provisions for withdrawals. The only way a person could recover his money before the organization was terminated was to leave the association—and even this required one month's notice and a penalty fee.

When a sufficient fund had been accumulated, the trustees announced at the following meeting that

they would be prepared to advance money . . . not to exceed the sum of five hundred dollars on any share. [A shareholder or shareholders interested in a loan decided] what premium he or they were willing to give for the same [and the loan went] to the member offering the highest sum.[28]

27 *Ibid.,* p. 40.
28 *Ibid.,* p. 42.

The loan was to be used only for

the purpose of erecting a dwelling or purchasing one [within an area
not more] than five miles from the market house in the Borough of
Frankford [and not outside of] the County of Philadelphia.[29]

The first loan—which was granted to a member who bid a
premium of $10—was for $375; in most cases, however, the full
$500 was borrowed on each share.[30] After receiving the loan,
the shareholder made monthly payments of 6 per cent interest
on the principal in addition to his regular monthly dues payments of $2.50. When the fund again reached $500, the trustees
announced that bids would be accepted for the next loan. This
continued until every member had received a loan. Then the
remaining money was divided among the shareholders (taking
account of amounts still due on outstanding loans), and on
January 11, 1841, the first Oxford Provident was terminated.

Other Early Building and Loan Associations in the United States

The need for home loans grew wherever the factory system
developed, and it is not surprising that the building and loan
association movement spread rapidly as industrialization moved
across the United States.

News of the Oxford Provident was carried by word of mouth
and by circulation of the Frankford newspaper. As it became
clear that it was successfully performing its intended functions,
other towns in the immediate area began forming similar organizations. It has been estimated that by 1840 there were more
than fifty building and loan associations in the Philadelphia
region alone.[31] In addition, the people of Frankford were so
enthusiastic about the accomplishments of their association that

---

29 *Ibid.*

30 Receiving a loan was not as simple as merely bidding the highest premium.
Each borrower had to be declared eligible by a building committee that checked
such things as the value of his property, his title, and his ability to repay the
loan. Even this did not assure repayments, however; Comly Rich, the first man
to get a loan, fell so far behind on his repayments that the association ultimately
confiscated his property and sold it by auction.

31 Seymour Dexter, *Cooperative Savings and Loan Associations* (New York:
Appleton-Century, 1889), p. 43.

a second and much larger Oxford Provident was started on January 30, 1841, just nineteen days after the first one was terminated.[32]

News of the Frankford organization traveled to more distant communities, and people from other areas came to learn about the association. In 1836, for example—when the first Oxford Provident was only five years old—a delegation came from Brooklyn. Upon returning home, this group started the second building and loan association in the United States—the Brooklyn Building and Mutual Loan Association.

As the population moved westward and as the number of wage earners increased, the demand for building and loan associations grew. The dates on the map below indicate the years in which the first building and loan association was started in each

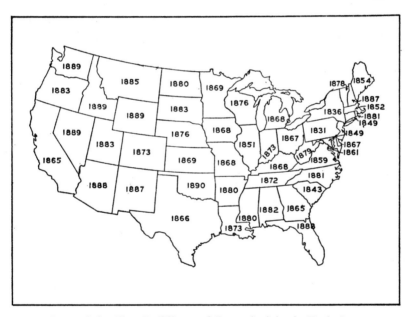

Date of the First Building and Loan Activity in Each State
Source: Bodfish, *History*.

[32] Accounts of the second Oxford Provident and the spread of building and loan associations across the United States can be found in Bodfish, *History*, pp. 75–96, and Bodfish and Theobald, pp. 39–50.

state. As might be expected, the dates are closely related to the major population movements and settlement concentrations of the nineteenth century.

Figures for the number of organizations operating in any particular year of the movement's early expansion period are considerably less precise than the dates for the opening of the first organization in each state. Some estimates were made for specific cities, but according to Frank B. Sanborn, there was no systematic attempt to compile state or national figures until he did the job in 1888. That year, it was calculated that there were about "3,000, perhaps even 3,500, Cooperative Building and Loan Associations in the United States and [that] they provide for the investment, at any given time, of not less than $300,000,-000." [33] A subsequent study suggests that this estimate was probably low: in 1893, when the Bureau of Labor made its first nationwide count, it found 5,860 building and loan associations in full-time operation throughout the United States.[34]

[33] Frank B. Sanborn, "Cooperative Building Associations," *Publication of the American Social Science Associations*, September, 1888, p. 114.

[34] U.S. Bureau of Labor, *Ninth Annual Report, Commissioner of Labor* (Washington, D.C.: Government Printing Office, 1894), pp. 391–94.

2

Structural and Functional Convergence

As MUTUAL SAVINGS BANKS and savings and loan associations developed, their structures and functions became more and more alike. This process of convergence includes structural changes associated with chartering arrangements as well as the relationships of savers, borrowers, trustees, and directors to their respective institutions. The main functional changes are related to the methods of accepting savings and making loans.

FROM TERMINATING TO PERMANENT CHARTERS

Mutual savings banks have always operated under charters that permit self-perpetuating boards of trustees to continue operations without regard to the participation of any particular group of savers, borrowers, or officers, and without being limited by any specific terminal dates. The earliest building and loan associations, on the other hand, operated under charters that were terminated as soon as every member had received and repaid a loan.

Early in the building and loan association movement it became clear that terminating plans were not well suited to the financial needs of growing communities. In most situations, each new group of settlers had to organize its own association. Even in cases where individuals were permitted to join after an association had started, initiation fees were used to equalize the amounts paid in, and these increased with the age of the organization until they became prohibitively large. Furthermore, toward the end of the life of each terminating association it became more and more difficult to match the inflow of savings with the demand for loans; idle funds accumulated, and income was lost.[1] Because of these and related shortcomings, there was considerable incentive to search for more flexible chartering arrangements.

Serial Charters [2]

The essential structural difference between terminating and serial charters was that, instead of permitting the issuance of just one group (or series) of shares and requiring termination when all loans had been repaid, the serial charter allowed each association to offer a new group of shares whenever the demand for membership was sufficiently large. Operations continued as long as at least one series remained outstanding. In the early serial associations, each new group of shares was managed and retired separately; but at some point, this custom usually evolved into the practice of treating the total inflow and outflow of savings as one large account.

The most obvious advantage of a serial plan was that operations remained comparatively simple, while at the same time a structure was provided for a continuing existence. New settlers

---

[1] Because of this problem, most early building and loan associations were terminated before all loans were repaid, with appropriate arrangements for the dispersal of savings being made when the final fund was divided. As one historian notes: "The terminating plan is very simple and seems easy of accomplishment. Practice, however, proves that it is seldom, if ever, carried out to the agreed point of termination, the difficulty being that, after the fourth or fifth year, the accumulating capital increases beyond the demand for it. . . . This is a natural and a certain result of a plan based on one issue of stock." Edmund Wrigley, *How to Manage Building Associations* (Philadelphia: J. K. Simon, 1880), pp. 24–25.

[2] The transition from terminating to serial plans took place between 1854, when the Third Oxford Provident was started under a serial charter, and the turn of the century. As early as 1889, one historian was able to observe that "the single series, or terminating plan, had been almost wholly replaced, and almost all associations were being formed on the serial plans." Seymour Dexter, *Cooperative Savings and Loan Associations* (New York: Appleton-Century, 1889), p. 74.

Serial plans remained the dominant type of chartering arrangement until the 1920s and 1930s when they were almost entirely replaced by permanent plans. See Horace F. Clark and Frank A. Chase, *Elements of the Modern Building and Loan Association* (New York: The Macmillan Company, 1925), p. 453.

were able to join established groups each time a sufficient number wanted home financing. In addition, serial charters permitted a continuity of bookkeeping and management not possible under terminating charters.

Despite these improvements, however, many problems remained. For instance, every member still had to join the organization as part of a group and to remain until his particular series was terminated; all savings had to be deposited and withdrawn on a contractual basis—once a series was started, penalty fees were imposed for deviating from the size and frequency of the required payments; both savers and borrowers still had membership obligations and ownership liabilities. To eliminate at least some of these rigidities, serial plans began to be changed almost as soon as they were introduced, and the ultimate result was the development of permanent charters.

Permanent Charters [3]

Under early permanent plans (or Dayton plans as they were first called), *each* share was treated as a separate series. Anyone could open an account at any time, make the required number

[3] The first building and loan associations in the United States to be incorporated under charters providing for permanent existences were organized in Charleston, South Carolina, in the early 1840s. Evidence indicates that, although the founders were familiar with previously formed terminating institutions, they founded their organizations under permanent charters because they wanted a plan "by which an individual is enabled to enter on the same footing with original members." For a history of these early institutions, see Reverend Cox, *Mutual Benefit Building and Loan Associations: Their History, Principles, and Plan of Operations* (Charleston: Brown and Co., 1852).

Even though these groups were started in the earliest stages of this nation's building and loan association movement, there is no indication that they influenced the chartering arrangements of any subsequent institutions. Not until the early 1880s, when Judge A. A. Winters returned from England and helped form the Mutual Home and Savings Association of Dayton, Ohio, did the idea of permanent charters begin to spread rapidly. For an account of the events leading to the formation of the first permanent building and loan association in Dayton, Ohio, and the subsequent spread of permanent charters, see Morton Bodfish, ed., *History of Building and Loan in the United States* (Chicago: United States Building and Loan League, 1931), pp. 93–99.

Nothing about a permanent charter guarantees that the operations of the organization will necessarily continue any longer than those of a group formed under a terminating or serial plan. The permanent charter is, of course, only permissive.

of monthly payments, and—if he had not taken out a loan in the interim—withdraw the full value of his savings when his series matured. In addition, he received any dividend that the directors may have declared for his type of share. To accommodate the individuals who were continually joining and leaving the organization, building and loan associations were permitted to operate under boards of directors who served terms that were unrelated to the participation of any particular group of savers or borrowers, and whose terms had no specific terminal date. By the end of World War II almost all savings and loan associations were operating under permanent charters.

EVOLUTION OF THE DEPOSITOR [4]

Savers with mutual savings banks have always been called depositors. As such, they have always been creditors of their respective institutions, legally entitled to share all distributed profits and to have their withdrawal requests honored upon demand.[5] Borrowers, on the other hand, have always been debtors to the institutions from which they received loans. In an operating mutual savings bank, neither savers nor borrowers have ever been members or owners in any legal or functional sense.[6]

People with savings in, or loans from, early building and loan associations, on the other hand, were both members and owners of their respective organizations, and in many cases this is still true.[7] Over the decades, however, many legal and structural

[4] See pp. 38–42 for a discussion of the depositing process.

[5] Thirty- to ninety-day statutory notice periods may be required, although they rarely have been.

[6] For a discussion of the creditor-depositor relation to mutual savings banks and for references to related legal cases, see John J. Redfield, "Savings Banks and Savings and Loan Associations, the Past and the Future," Address before the Committee on Savings and Loan Associations of the Banking and Business Law Section of the American Bar Association, Washington, D.C., August 27, 1960, pp. 6–9.

[7] Exceptions to this are savings and loan associations with permanent, guaranteed, or capital stock. In these organizations, ownership rights are usually reserved for the stockholders; savers and borrowers have only creditor rights and debtor obligations, just as in mutual savings banks. These types of savings and loan associations are discussed below.

changes have resulted in savers and borrowers being treated as creditors and debtors. Perhaps even more important, practical arrangements have evolved to the point where most savings and loan association shareholders expect these creditor and debtor relationships to be honored.[8]

In early building and loan associations, to recapitulate briefly, all shareholders were members and owners in a practical as well as a legal sense. Each participant was required to attend a certain number of meetings each year, or he incurred a fine; he was eligible to vote for the directors and other officers and was expected to participate at one time or another on one or more of the committees that performed the actual operations. With respect to ownership, these associations were partnerships in which all participants assumed unlimited liability for the actions of the group. Thus, each shareholder had an immediate and pressing reason for participating in the operations and decisions of his organization. But as building and loan associations responded to the evolving needs of borrowers and savers, so did the practical and legal relationships change between shareowners and their respective institutions.

Participation

Most building and loan associations were organized in regions where there were shortages of capital, and it was not long before

[8] There is a vast literature of court cases in which shareholders of savings and loan associations have been legally identified, and treated, as creditors and debtors. Citing a few examples, Redfield writes: "Certainly, cases involving mutual savings and loan institutions dealing with taxation, garnishment and gifts have treated the share accounts as deposits rather than as shares of stock. In *Atwood* v. *Dumas*, a garnishment case, Mr. Justice Holmes stated: 'It does not follow, because the defendant is a member [of a savings and loan association] that she may not be a creditor in respect to her money paid in,' and in *Bell* v. *Bakertown Savings Assns.*, a gift case, the Pennsylvania court concluded, in the case of a mutual savings association, 'Under the above recited facts the savings account is analogous to a bank account rather than to shares of stocks and is to be governed by the familiar principles which are applicable to bank accounts.' "

For additional citations, see Redfield, pp. 6–7, and for further discussion of the legal arrangements among savers, borrowers, and savings and loan associations, see Horace Russell and William Prather, "Legal Aspects of Savings Accounts," United States Savings and Loan League, *Legal Bulletin*, Vol. XXV, No. 1 (September, 1959), and William Prather, "The Modern Savings Account Concept," United States Savings and Loan League, *Legal Bulletin*, Vol. XXIII, No. 47 (May, 1957).

many groups began to realize the advantages of permitting individuals to maintain savings accounts without at the same time requiring them to accept loans. Before this type of arrangement could be popularized, however, provisions had to be developed for limiting the liability of each shareholder at least to the amount in his account. This was accomplished with contractual agreements made when a share was issued. With respect to borrowers, on the other hand, once it became standard to require a residential mortgage as collateral for a loan, it became customary to limit the borrower's liability to the size of his debt.

As provisions for the separation of savers and borrowers and for limited liability became more common, the thrift services of building and loan associations became increasingly attractive to individuals whose primary motive for saving was to receive the highest return consistent with the desired standards of safety, liquidity, and convenience. Most savers, especially those with limited liability, were not attracted by the idea of having to attend meetings or otherwise to participate in administrative functions, especially when such participation was not being required by competing savings institutions.

As building and loan associations continued trying to increase their savings inflows, the desirability of eliminating as many savers' obligations as possible became apparent. In most cases, a form of corporate government was developed that allowed shareowners legally to remain members and owners while delegating all of the operational responsibilities to elected directors and officers. By this arrangement, as one author observes:

The control by savings account holders is *limited to a set of rules* which the members prescribe for the selection and instruction of their representatives, to resolutions which the members may pass to guide their representatives, and to the election of directors at the annual membership meeting.[9]

With the development of the practice of honoring all withdrawal requests upon demand, even the limited involvement of voting for directors or attending annual meetings ceased to have

[9] Leon T. Kendall, *The Savings and Loan Business* (Englewood Cliffs, N.J.: Prentice-Hall, 1962), p. 29 (emphasis added).

any practical significance for the average shareholder—except in a few situations where the safety of the savings seemed actually to be in danger. Under provisions for discretionary withdrawals, if the saver had any dissatisfaction with the way the organization was being managed, he simply terminated his relationship by withdrawing his funds. In addition, there are legal precedents for permitting incumbent directors to disfranchise dissatisfied savers by returning their money if they refuse to leave the organization voluntarily.[10]

Despite these legal and operational changes, however, saver participation (primarily by voting) increased in the 1930s as many shareowners tried to salvage at least part of their funds from failing and otherwise unsafe savings and loan associations.[11] As an outgrowth of depression experience, however, safety and liquidity conditions in the savings and loan association industry were changed so fundamentally that throughout the post-World War II period it has been customary to honor all withdrawal requests as presented, and once again shareowner participation has become virtually unknown.[12]

[10] For example, see *Daurelle* v. *Traders Federal Savings and Loan Assn. of Parkersburg*, 104 S.W. 2d 320 (1958).

In addition to the observations above, it is frequently alleged that the influence of an individual saver or borrower on the management of his organization varies inversely with the size of the group and that the interest that the ordinary shareholder has in exercising his ownership and management rights diminishes as his institution grows. Over a quarter of a century ago, for example, using 5,000 shareholders to typify a "large" organization, the leading historians of the building and loan association movement noted: "Obviously, in an institution with 5,000 investors interested in the safety of their savings and a reasonable return thereon, the individual shareholder and investor takes only a passive interest; and the integrity and capacity of the management as trustees, plus the appropriateness of statutory restriction, are depended upon for the competent determination of the year-to-year policies and the proper control over the affairs of the institution." Morton Bodfish and A. D. Theobald, *Savings and Loan Principles* (Englewood Cliffs, N.J.: Prentice-Hall, 1940), p. 73.

[11] An account of the number of savings and loan associations failing in the 1930s appears on p. 119.

[12] Since 1945, for example, both state- and federally-chartered savings and loan associations have had to meet minimum liquidity requirements, as well as regulations limiting investments and other operational procedures that have been considerably more stringent (and more carefully enforced) than those of the 1930s. Moreover, all Federal Home Loan Bank System members (holding 98.4 per cent of the industry's assets in 1964) have been permitted to borrow up to 50 per cent of their savings liabilities when necessary to meet withdrawal re-

In fact, since 1945, savings and loan associations have generally been so well prepared to meet all withdrawal demands that it has become increasingly common for officials of this industry to consider legal arrangements such as "due notice" agreements and rotation plans not only unnecessary but actually competitively disadvantageous. Many savings and loan association executives and Federal Home Loan Bank System officials have advocated the removal of all restrictions on the repayment of savings accounts, with the sole exception of a 60-day statutory notice period that could be evoked if an organization needed additional time to acquire liquidity.[13] This has already been done for state-chartered organizations in certain states.[14] As these arrangements become increasingly common, more and more savers with savings and loan associations will be placed into creditor relationships closely resembling those that have always existed between depositors and mutual savings banks.

Ownership

With respect to ownership, similarities between savers in mutual savings banks and nonstock savings and loan associations have always been evident. As Lintner has pointed out, the two types of institutions have always been "equally mutual in terms of ownership of assets and distribution of earnings to depositors and shareowners."[15] In both cases, all net earnings must either

---

quests. As a group, these provisions have made it possible for all legally operated savings and loan associations to meet all withdrawal requests upon demand. Furthermore, formation of the Federal Savings and Loan Insurance Corporation (insuring 96.2 per cent of the industry's assets in 1964) guarantees the return of savings up to $10,000 per account even in case of default, thus eliminating the major cause of panic withdrawals. These and other post-depression developments are discussed in chapter 7.

[13] A spokesman for the savings and loan association industry has recently observed: "The safety features built into the economy and into the savings and loan business during the last generation have tended to reinforce the premise that the rotation plan could be eliminated without harm, a conviction held by a good many savings and loan executives and Federal Home Loan Bank System officials. In fact, there is sentiment at the federal level as well as in a number of states for removing rotation from the settlement provisions in savings and loan account contracts." Kendall, *The Savings and Loan Business*, p. 76.

[14] For example, see the *New York Banking Law*, Art. X, par. 390.

[15] John Lintner, *Mutual Savings Banks in the Savings and Mortgage Markets* (Boston: Harvard University, Graduate School of Business Administration, 1948), p. 54.

be distributed to the savers on a prorata basis or added to reserves for the greater protection of the savings accounts. In the event that either type of organization is terminated, liquidation procedures require that the savers receive their funds after the sale of assets and after all other debts have been paid. They also receive a prorata share of any remaining surplus. The similarity of claims in organizations affiliated with the Federal Deposit Insurance Corporation or the Federal Savings and Loan Insurance Corporation is even more apparent. In the event that any insured institution is liquidated or declared in default, savings up to a predetermined amount are equally protected.

The preceding discussion does not apply to savings and loan associations with either permanent, or guaranteed, shares or capital stock. With few exceptions, these organizations have *always* treated their savers as depositors and creditors and their borrowers as debtors. In this respect, these institutions have always been similar to mutual savings banks.

When an organization is formed with permanent shares, for example, a certain class of securities is created to establish a fund for guaranteeing the principal of "regular" savings accounts and for providing proceeds for paying dividends until the institution begins to generate earnings. This is similar to the capital fund established at the founding of a mutual savings bank. Holders of the permanent shares typically reserve all ownership and membership rights for themselves. As one study of this type of organization observes:

... it was generally provided by the article of incorporation that the majority of the directors shall always be selected from the capital guarantee [or permanent] stockholders; [but] in practice, it is customary to select *all* of the directors from those who by their subscription for this class of stock have assumed the responsibilities involved.[16]

In savings and loan associations with capital stock outstand-

[16] Holtby R. Myers, "The California Guarantee Stock Plan," *American Building Association News*, XLI (December, 1921), 552 (emphasis added). For additional information on the way permanent, or guarantee, share organizations operate, see Henry S. Rosenthal and Robert B. Jacoby, *Cyclopedia of Federal Savings and Loan Associations* (Cincinnati: American Building Association News, 1939).

ing, as in commercial banks and almost all other types of capital stock organizations, stockholders have *all* of the membership and ownership rights and obligations. In these institutions, borrowers are debtors and savers are depositor-creditors, treated just as they have always been treated in mutual savings banks.[17]

TRUSTEES AND DIRECTORS

Mutual savings banks have always been supervised by boards of trustees that have been either self-perpetuating or selected by self-perpetuating boards of incorporators. The original trustees of each group were usually its founders as well as the individuals who provided its initial reserves. In the formative period of each organization, the trustees typically managed the operations personally, but as the institutions grew, it generally became necessary for trustees to appoint full-time officers to oversee daily activities. Today, the laws of some states require that the trustees be selected for definite periods—usually three to five years—and a few states limit the number of terms that may be served. But usually the service of a mutual savings bank trustee is limited only by a mandatory retirement age.

Consistent with the history and philosophy of mutual savings banking, trustees have always been required to maintain strictly fiduciary positions with respect to their organizations and the depositors. Other than nominal compensation for attending board meetings or for working on special committees, they are prohibited by law from receiving any financial benefit, either directly or collaterally, from the operations of their organizations.[18] In practice, these restrictions have been strictly interpreted and rigorously applied.

The obligations and duties of early building and loan association directors (or trustees, as they were first called) were similar

[17] At the end of 1964, approximately 12 per cent of the 6,325 savings and loan associations had capital stock outstanding, and between one quarter to one half of the industry's assets were in either permanent share or capital stock organizations.

[18] This does not enjoin mutual savings bank trustees who are also lawyers or officers of their organizations from receiving compensation for services rendered in these other capacities.

in many respects to those of the mutual savings bank trustees. For example, the directors were fully responsible for managing the affairs of their organizations, a task they performed without compensation. As the groups got larger, they had the duty of appointing full-time officers to handle the daily functions, while they continued overseeing the operations.

Unlike mutual savings bank trustees, however, the boards of directors of early building and loan associations were not self-perpetuating. Directors were elected to serve for fixed terms— usually one or two years—and it was not uncommon for them to be declared ineligible to succeed themselves. When the organizations were small, directors were usually elected by members who knew them personally and who considered them the most likely people to do the job well. If they failed to live up to this trust, they could be replaced in comparatively short order.[19] In most cases, however, this is no longer true.

Even though most directors continue to be elected, there is a *de facto* self-perpetuation of the boards of directors resulting from the failure of most shareholders to vote. Consequently, a comparatively small group typically retains control of the administration by voting its own shares and the organization's proxies as well.[20] The executive vice-president of the United States Savings and Loan League has acknowledged that "in practice, the savings and loan board [of directors] may be essentially a self-perpetuating body." [21]

As long as competing institutions do not require savers to participate actively in their administration, and as long as sav-

[19] Directors of savings and loan associations that were started with permanent shares are usually exceptions to this rule. These boards of directors are typically self-perpetuating.

[20] The fact that almost all savings and loan association boards of directors are self-perpetuating has been well known for so long that almost a quarter of a century ago the industry's foremost historians thought it appropriate to suggest: "Possibly, the savings and loan business, *instead of maintaining the fiction of popular rule,* would do well to consider a more realistic approach and adopt the trustee system. . . . The ideal of a public service, financial corporation operated for the benefit of all interested parties does not require the preservation of a legal fiction which is neither practical nor necessary." Bodfish and Theobald, p. 74 (emphasis added).

[21] Norman Strunk, "A Federal System of Mutual Savings Banks?" *Savings and Loan News,* LXXXVI, No. 5 (May, 1963), 40.

ings can be withdrawn upon request, it is likely that shareholders will continue to be passive in the management of savings and loan associations. Only in times of the most unusual stress, or in the event of failure to meet withdrawal demands, have members been known to unseat incumbent directors against their will. Since the 1930s these cases have been extremely rare.

As the savings and loan association industry evolved, it became increasingly common for directors not only to receive compensation for services performed as officers and lawyers of their respective organizations—as did mutual savings bank trustees—but also to profit from positions or financial interests with other organizations to which business was directed from their savings and loan associations. In addition, many received salaries as directors. Thus, the businessmen who formed savings and loan associations—unlike those who founded mutual savings banks—were often motivated by strong profit incentives. In many cases, they needed a financing source as builders or welcomed opportunities to earn fees as lawyers, real estate agents, or insurance brokers.[22]

These differences should not, however, be allowed to obscure the basic similarities between the boards of trustees and directors: two types of essentially self-perpetuating, supervisory bodies responsible ultimately to savers who can withdraw their funds upon request and to borrowers seeking loans at the lowest possible cost.

FUNCTIONAL CONVERGENCE: MUTUAL SAVINGS BANK DEPOSITS

The process by which mutual savings banks handle savings has remained virtually unchanged since The Bank for Savings in the City of New York was started almost a century and a half ago. Although a few early institutions required that savings be

---

[22] The recent movement of savings and loan associations into suburban areas—discussed in chapters 4 through 8—may well have been stimulated as much by a desire to take advantage of the growth of housing markets in these areas as by a wish to supply deposit facilities as savers moved out of the central portions of the cities.

set aside systematically, most have always allowed deposits and withdrawals to be made in amounts and at times selected by savers.[23] Contractual savings such as Christmas funds, accounts for the purchase of government bonds, or payments on life insurance premiums have never been more than a minor part of total deposits.

Interest payments have usually been declared quarterly or semiannually by the trustees. In most cases, rates are the same for all depositors, although in recent years increased use has been made of split rates—with higher returns being paid on funds deposited more than a year. In addition, some use has been made of "notice accounts," with higher rates going to savers who precede withdrawal demands with a 30-day written notice; but again, this is a relatively minor part of all mutual savings bank deposits. More than 98 per cent of all such deposits are currently insured up to $15,000 per account by the Federal Deposit Insurance Corporation, the Massachusetts Mutual Savings Central Fund, or both.

As a result of the desire to promote thrift among people of modest means, many early mutual savings banks restricted the size of their accounts to comparatively small deposits from individuals and larger amounts from nonprofit institutions only. Today, although the ability of mutual savings banks to handle large deposits safely and efficiently is not questioned, and although incomes are constantly rising, many of these limitations still exist. Moreover, in at least six mutual savings bank states— including four of the five with the largest amounts in mutual savings bank deposits—restraints are now imposed by law. In New York, for example, deposits are limited to $25,000 per account ($15,000 until 1965) and to individuals and nonprofit organizations. This type of legislation, although it may have served a purpose many years ago, reduces the ability of mutual savings banks to compete effectively with other savings institutions, while providing no discernible benefits to small savers.

23 Legally, a 30- to 90-day written notice may be requested before withdrawal demands must be honored, but most mutual savings banks have rarely, if ever, imposed this requirement. For a discussion of the 1930s, when written notice was occasionally required, see p. 120.

Regardless of restrictions on the size of accounts and the fact that procedures for making deposits and withdrawals have remained virtually unchanged throughout the industry's history, the flexibility, safety, liquidity, and returns of mutual savings bank deposits have made them sufficiently adaptable to satisfy the needs of an ever-increasing number of savers.

SAVINGS ACCOUNTS IN SAVINGS AND LOAN ASSOCIATIONS

Unlike the situation with mutual savings banks, changes began to take place almost immediately in the functional relationship between savers and building and loan associations, particularly after the development of serial and permanent plans. Most of these changes are not clearly documented; but based on fragmentary information, the following appears to have happened. A member joined an association and began making savings payments, fully intending to accept the loan to which he was entitled when funds became available. Then, after the organization had been operating for a number of months or years, he changed his mind. In the meantime, additional members had joined on new series and wanted loans as soon as possible. They were permitted to use some of the funds that had been saved by earlier shareholders, and eventually they repaid the borrowed funds with interest. When the series of an earlier member (who had chosen not to receive a loan) was terminated, he was allowed to withdraw his principal as well as a portion of the interest payments, fines, and service charges that had accumulated. Thus, the separation of savers and borrowers developed as an initial step in the evolution of the modern savings account.

As building and loan associations grew, it became easier and more common to accept savings from people who had no intention of requesting loans. New savings services were created, and most of the accompanying functional changes can be inferred from a description of the savings plans themselves.

The types of savings procedures that were tried are almost as numerous as the number of building and loan associations. But three were particularly common and each was an important forerunner of the type of savings account most widely used today.[24] Of course, building and loan associations switched from one plan to another at different times; furthermore, it was, and still is, not uncommon for an organization to offer three or four kinds of savings accounts simultaneously.

The *installment share* was one of the earliest plans permitting a member to save without also being required to accept a loan. Under this arrangement, an individual subscribed to one or more shares, either alone or as part of a group, and made payments at periodic intervals. Each share had a fixed value and a predetermined maturity date, but no provisions for early withdrawals. Interest was the difference between the maturity value and the total savings payments. Some of the later installment plans have provisions for allowing withdrawals before maturity.

In response to the expanding demand for loans, attempts were made to increase the flexibility of savings services, and the *optional share account* was one of the earlier results. In many respects, optional share accounts are similar to installment shares—in fact, they are called installment shares in some states—but the fundamental difference is that with early optional shares savers were permitted to make payments in amounts and at times of their own choosing until the face value of the share was reached. In case of premature withdrawals, interest payments and occasionally part of the principal were forfeited. In later optional accounts, withdrawals were permitted, but only after the saver gave "due notice."

A more recent development, and a direct precursor of the modern savings account, was the *full-paid share,* sometimes called the "paid-up" or "income" share. This type of account usually had a face value of $50 or $100 which was generally paid when the share was issued. Savers then had the alternative of receiving interest in cash at regular intervals or of allowing it to accumulate. In either case, with the earliest type of full-paid

24 For descriptions of other types of share accounts, see Clark and Chase, pp. 63–78, and Henry S. Rosenthal, *Cyclopedia of Building and Loan Associations* (Cincinnati: American Building Association News, 1939), pp. 117–18, 190–95.

share, written notice was required before any principal could be withdrawn.

As the number of shareholders in any particular building and loan association increased, it became feasible to operate under the banking principle of trying to honor all withdrawal requests as they were presented. During the 1920s and 1930s, many building and loan associations switched to this procedure, simultaneously changing their names to savings and loan associations to underscore the importance of their savings services. By the end of World War II, almost all of these institutions had abandoned the practice of requiring "due notice" and had started permitting the amounts and timing of deposits and withdrawals to be completely at the savers' discretion. Thus, the current savings account was adopted. By the 1940s almost all savings and loan associations were providing fundamentally the same savings services as those offered by mutual savings banks.[25]

MUTUAL SAVINGS BANK ASSETS

In the early years of their existence, mutual savings banks

put all their money into government and state bonds, in accordance with their charters which directed that the funds be put into "stocks created or issued under and by virtue of the laws of the United States or of the State, *and in no other way.*" [26]

[25] Referring to the final stages of this convergence, the executive vice-president of the United States Savings and Loan League has indicated that to a certain extent at least the similarity of savings services between savings and loan associations and mutual savings banks is a direct result of the former consciously copying the methods of the latter. For example, he observes: "As for actual operations or workings on the savings side, there is little difference between the modern savings and loan associations and the savings bank. In fact, our [current savings account] was tailored essentially after the type of account offered by the savings banks and became the substitute for the installment share account, the prepaid share account, and the full-paid share type of savings account offered by our business prior to the depression." Strunk, "Federal System," p. 40.

The following excerpt also attests to the functional similarity of the savings services of these two industries as well as to their continuing convergence.

"Newark, N.J.—United States Savings Bank here announced Tuesday it is setting up a computer network which, in addition to its own offices, will process instantaneously the savings accounts of four savings banks and one savings and loan association in five New Jersey cities." *American Banker*, September 22, 1965, p. 1.

By 1962, however, a study of mutual savings banks was able to note:

As a result of their *basic orientation toward mortgage lending* . . . savings banks have sought to channel a large portion of their funds into mortgages. Through the years except during World War II and early postwar periods, mortgages have constituted the largest single category of savings bank assets.[27]

The following section discusses the major legal and operational changes in the investment practices of mutual savings banks that ultimately led to their "basic orientation toward mortgage lending," the traditional investment function of savings and loan associations.

Investments before 1900

When The Bank for Savings in the City of New York was organized in 1819, its charter permitted investments only in U.S. Government and New York State bonds.[28] These securities were considered appropriately safe, liquid, and remunerative for the needs of mutual savings banking; at that time they provided annual yields of about 5 per cent. The very next year, 1820, The Bank for Savings requested and was granted the right to lend money to the City of New York, thus establishing the precedent for adding municipal bonds to the investment alternatives of mutual savings banks. At the same time, permission to purchase local real estate mortgages was requested and denied.[29]

---

26 Franklin J. Sherman, *Modern Story of Mutual Savings Banks* (New York: Little and Ives, 1934), p. 70 (emphasis added). This applied to the earliest mutual savings banks in New York, Massachusetts, Pennsylvania, Connecticut, and Rhode Island.

27 National Association of Mutual Savings Banks, *Mutual Savings Banking: Basic Characteristics and Role in the National Economy* (Englewood Cliffs, N.J.: Prentice-Hall, 1962), p. 100 (emphasis added).

28 Examples from experiences in New York are used throughout this section to illustrate important legal changes that were subsequently adopted throughout the industry.

29 With the inflation during and after the War of 1812, the financial panic of 1819, and the ensuing depression there were wide fluctuations in real estate prices. Thus, it is not hard to see why residential mortgages were considered too risky for the portfolios of mutual savings banks. And the same is true for corporate securities.

As mutual savings banks grew in number and size, their investment problems became increasingly acute. A time came when it was apparent that, if they remained confined solely to government securities (assuming there were enough to be had for everybody), they would be unable to meet their operating expenses and pay an attractive return to their depositors. New outlets were sought.

The next investment breakthrough came in 1827 when the New York legislature amended the charter of The Bank for Savings to allow purchases of public securities offered by the state of Ohio.[30] Two years later, in 1829, the Seamen's Savings Bank was given permission to purchase the securities of Pennsylvania as well as those of Ohio and New York. Thus, precedents were established for allowing mutual savings banks to acquire the securities of other states.

The next year, 1830, The Bank for Savings once again applied for and this time received permission to make what was essentially a loan collateralized by a real estate mortgage. It was authorized to lend money to "the Public School Society of New York on satisfactory real security." [31] A still broader precedent for investing in real estate mortgages, including those on private homes, was set the following year when the Poughkeepsie Savings Bank was authorized to make loans on "bonds and mortgages on real estate double the value of the sum loaned." In 1832 this privilege was extended to the Brooklyn Savings Bank and subsequently to many other mutual savings banks as well.

Going back one year, in 1831, The Bank for Savings had requested and received the right to build a surplus for the protection of deposits. Originally, this was not to exceed 3 per cent of deposits; in 1839, the maximum was raised to 10 per cent. Thus, in little more than a decade and a half, precedents were established for investing in four major types of assets: federal,

[30] In 1827 the Albany Savings Bank was permitted to invest in the stocks of commercial banks in Albany and Troy, but this right was subsequently withdrawn.

[31] Many statements in the next few pages rely upon information found in the books by Keyes and Sherman, as well as in Weldon Welfling, *Savings Banking in New York State* (Durham, N.C.: Duke University Press, 1939).

state, and municipal bonds as well as mortgages on public buildings and private homes.

In ensuing years, the charters of New York mutual savings banks were liberalized to allow loans based on personal security (1842) and on the securities of any city (1849), county (1857), or town (1863) in the state.[32] In addition, certain corporate stocks—primarily of railroads and utility companies—were authorized in the 1870s and 1880s.

Throughout most of the 1880s and 1890s, recessionary pressures kept bond prices high, and for many mutual savings banks, real estate mortgages became the most attractive investment among the legal alternatives. From 1875 through 1890, mortgages rose from less than 20 per cent to more than 40 per cent of assets in New York mutual savings banks, and similar increases were experienced in almost all other mutual savings bank states. From the turn of this century to the present, except for the World War II years, residential mortgages have been the largest single investment category of both the mutual savings bank and the savings and loan association industries.

Investments, 1900–1945

The predominant features of mutual savings bank investments from 1900 to 1945 were (1) a constant increase in the range of legal alternatives within each of the major categories previously discussed, (2) a long-term increase in residential mortgages as a percentage of total investments, (3) a growing investment in nonresidential mortgages, including commercial and industrial property as well as schools, churches, and other community buildings, (4) a shifting among asset groups as conditions in capital and equity markets changed, and (5) a tendency for mortgages as a percentage of assets to rise and fall with the building cycle.[33] The following paragraphs trace a few of

[32] A detailed breakdown of investment changes from 1819 through 1864 appears in Sherman, pp. 71–75.

[33] For more complete histories of mutual savings bank investment policies and practices since 1900, see Lintner (concentrating primarily on Massachusetts), Welfling (focusing almost entirely on New York), Raymond W. Goldsmith, *Financial Intermediaries in the American Economy since 1900* (Princeton, N.J.: Prince-

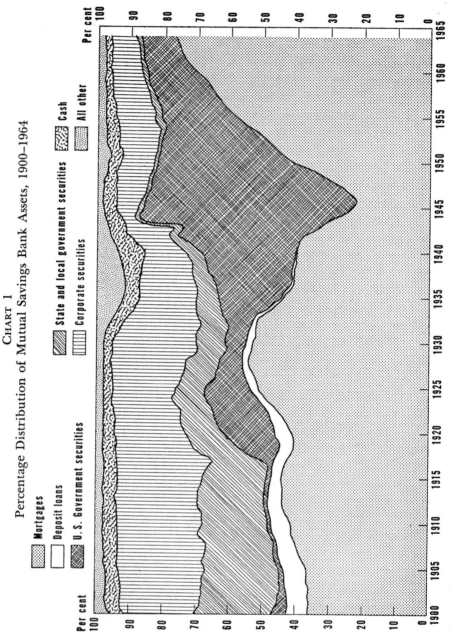

Chart 1

Percentage Distribution of Mutual Savings Bank Assets, 1900–1964

Mortgages

Deposit loans

U. S. Government securities

State and local government securities

Corporate securities

Cash

All other

Source: National Association of Mutual Savings Banks.

the more important investment changes in each decade of the twentieth century. (See Chart 1 for additional detail.)

The financial panic of 1907 appears to have been the dominant event influencing mutual savings bank investments prior to World War I. During that year, "while the values of marketable securities were scraping bottom, unquoted mortgage values were unaffected and borrowers continued their interest [payments]." [34] This encouraged mutual savings bankers to continue increasing their mortgage loans. As a proportion of assets, mortgages rose more than 1 per cent annually from 1907 to 1914.

The second decade brought World War I. U.S. Government bonds rose from less than 1 per cent of the industry's assets in 1917 to over 16 per cent in 1922. This advance was primarily at the expense of corporate securities. The industry's mortgage-to-asset ratio also fell moderately, from 43 per cent in 1917 to 40 per cent in 1920.

During the 1920s, mutual savings banks rapidly increased their mortgage loans as the prolonged housing and real estate boom combined with substantial increases in the use of external financing to push mortgage yields up to 6 per cent and above.[35] From 1920 to 1929, the industry's mortgage-to-asset ratio climbed from 41 to 55 per cent while its total assets rose from $5.8 billion to $9.9 billion. By 1930, mutual savings banks held over $4½ billion in residential mortgages and roughly $1 billion in loans on commercial, industrial, and community property.

From the stock market crash in October, 1929, to the end of

---

ton University Press, 1958), and W. H. Steiner, "Mutual Savings Banks," *Law and Contemporary Problems* (Durham, N.C.: Duke University School of Law, Winter, 1952). In addition, for a breakdown of mortgage and security investments, see the National Association of Mutual Savings Banks, *Mutual Savings Banking*, chapters 5–7, Saul B. Klaman, *The Postwar Residential Mortgage Market* (Princeton, N.J.: Princeton University Press, 1961), and National Association of Mutual Savings Banks, *Annual Report: Facts and Figures, 1966.* Also see Raymond W. Goldsmith, *A Study of Saving in the United States,* Vol. I (Princeton, N.J.: Princeton University Press, 1955).

[34] Welfling, p. 32.

[35] During this period, interest payments on most securities were comparatively low. Yields on short-term federal bonds, for example, fluctuated between 2½ to 3½ per cent.

World War II, the proportion of mutual savings bank assets in mortgages fell from 54 to 23 per cent. However, the reasons for this decline were not the same throughout the period.

In the early 1930s, a sharp reduction in building activity and in the demand for home financing resulted in substantial declines in mortgage yields. Most mutual savings banks stopped investing in residential mortgages, while many tried to liquidate existing holdings. With security prices falling, commercial banks closing, and unemployment mounting, property owners often found it impossible to make interest and principal payments on outstanding loans. In many cases, mutual savings banks felt forced to foreclose on the mortgages. In most of these situations, property could only be sold at substantially reduced prices, if at all; typically, it was frozen into the mutual savings banks' portfolios. (Note the increase in the "all other" category in Chart 1.)

The reduced attractiveness of mortgages was accompanied by similar declines in the desirability of corporate, state, and municipal securities.[36] As a result, all of these assets declined throughout the decade as a percentage of the industry's portfolio. Only U.S. Government securities and property acquired through foreclosures increased in relation to total assets.

In the late 1930s, residential construction and the demand for home financing revived. Mortgage yields rose. But unlike savings and loan associations, most mutual savings banks failed to reenter the mortgage market. In fact, as a percentage of the industry's portfolio, mortgages declined almost 1 per cent annually from 1935 to 1939. Commenting on this, John Lintner observes:

Even though the demands for mortgage credit in these years were relatively low, they were sufficiently large to enable other lenders to increase their portfolios during the period. The [mutual savings] banks could have loaned as much as other lenders and they could

[36] Mutual savings banks had started to reduce their holdings of state and municipal securities long before the depression decade. With the introduction of income tax, declining yields on these securities discounted their tax-exempt status; thus, these securities were of little advantage to the income-tax-exempt mutual savings banks.

have obtained business as their competitors did; their returns would have been high and virtually free from risk, and even on the loans which got into trouble the subsequent yield would have been higher than that available on government bonds purchased in the market. Nevertheless, the banks largely withdrew from the mortgage market, let their mortgage portfolios run off, and took the easy course of putting most available investment funds into government bonds.[37]

Despite changes that took place during the 1930s, the predominant assets held by both mutual savings banks and savings and loan associations at the beginning of World War II were residential mortgages and U.S. Government securities.

From 1940 through 1945, as demand for mortgage financing fell with the curtailment of private construction, almost all of the net savings gain and almost all loan repayments were invested in U.S. Government bonds. Thus, from 1930 through 1945, Government securities rose from 5 per cent of mutual savings bank assets to slightly over 60 per cent, while mortgages fell from 53 per cent to less than 25 per cent.

Investments since 1945

By the end of World War II, there were important similarities in the investment functions of mutual savings banks and savings and loan associations. Even though the former had a wider range of investment alternatives, 85 per cent of their assets were in mortgages and U.S. Government securities, compared to 91 per cent for the savings and loan association industry.

By 1945, mutual savings banks had reduced their state and municipal bonds to less than 2 per cent of assets. They had sold almost all of the property acquired by foreclosures during the 1930s—the "all other" category in Chart 1 had declined to less than 2 per cent. Cash, which had risen slightly during World War II, had fallen back into its traditional range of 2 to 4 per cent of assets; deposit loans had declined to less than 1 per cent. And all of these categories have remained at or below their 1945 levels down to the present.

[37] Lintner, p. 238.

Thus, during the post-World War II period, the major difference between the over-all asset structure of the mutual savings bank and savings and loan association industries was that the former held corporate securities (ranging from 3 per cent of assets in 1945 to 11 per cent in 1964), while this investment possibility was denied to most savings and loan associations.

For most of the post-1945 period, the prolonged boom in construction activity, the rapid turnover in housing, and the increased use of external financing kept mortgage yields generally higher than returns on other assets in which mutual savings banks might invest. Consequently, the dominant lending function of mutual savings banks during these years led to increased acquisition of both residential and nonresidential mortgages and the reduction of U.S. Government securities. While assets rose by $37.3 billion from 1946 through 1964, $36.1 billion (97 per cent) went into mortgages. Meanwhile, U.S. Government securities were reduced by $4.9 billion. Total mortgages rose from 25 per cent to about 75 per cent of assets.

As a result of their rapid shift back into mortgages, the investment practices of mutual savings banks became more than ever before like those of savings and loan associations. It has become standard procedure for both types of institutions to rely on mortgages as the primary source of income while holding U.S. Government securities largely for secondary liquidity.[38]

Thus, although covergence of their lending services is by no means as complete as convergence of their savings services, mutual savings banks and savings and loan associations have become increasingly similar in their investment functions throughout the post-1945 period, and currently their lending services resemble each other more closely than they do those of any other type of institution. As long as mortgage yields remain

[38] For discussions of the investment practices of mutual savings banks during the post-1945 period, see J. Brooke Willis, "Gross Flows of Funds Through Mutual Savings Banks," *Journal of Finance*, XV (May, 1960), 170–90, and National Association of Mutual Savings Banks, *Mutual Savings Banking*, pp. 100–173. For a year-by-year record of the net flow of funds from mutual savings banks into each of the major investment categories, see National Association of Mutual Savings Banks, *Annual Report: Facts and Figures, 1965*, p. 23.

generally higher than the returns on any of the other investment alternatives open to mutual savings banks, functional convergence can be expected to continue.

SAVINGS AND LOAN ASSOCIATION ASSETS

As previously noted, early building and loan associations accepted savings solely to provide members with financing for the purchase or construction of homes. In almost all cases, collateral was a mortgage on the property itself.

In the course of regular operations, every association found itself holding a second asset—the cash accumulated prior to making a loan or when there was no immediate demand for financing. Shareholders soon realized that some of this fund could be profitably lent to members on a short-term basis, with the savings balances themselves providing collateral. Thus, a third asset—share loans—was developed. By the turn of the twentieth century, as Chart 2 indicates, these loans constituted approximately 5 per cent of the industry's assets. As it became more usual to honor withdrawal demands upon request, this method of borrowing became less common. By 1940, share loans had fallen to less than 1 per cent of the industry's portfolio, and they have remained at this level ever since.

Building and loan associations also acquired real estate. Some, of course, was for business purposes, but residential and commercial property was also received through the foreclosure of mortgages. Throughout most of the twentieth century real estate fluctuated between 1 and 5 per cent of assets, the exception being in the 1930s when foreclosures rose sharply and property could not be profitably sold. Then the proportion of real estate to total assets increased rapidly, climbing above 20 per cent in 1935. Most of this property was sold (much of it at a profit) during the early 1940s. Since then, real estate acquired by foreclosure has constituted less than 1 per cent of the industry's portfolio.

The last major type of asset in which savings and loan associations are permitted to invest is U.S. Government securities.

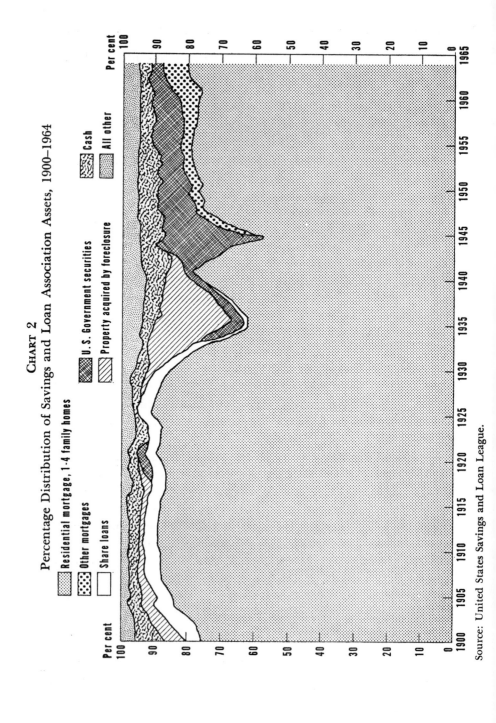

CHART 2

Percentage Distribution of Savings and Loan Association Assets, 1900–1964

Residential mortgage, 1-4 family homes
Other mortgages
Share loans
U. S. Government securities
Property acquired by foreclosure
Cash
All other

Source: United States Savings and Loan League.

These were first purchased during World War I but remained a relatively small part of the industry's portfolio until the early 1930s, when the Federal Home Loan Bank System imposed minimum liquidity requirements on its members and allowed these requirements to be met partially with U.S. Government securities. In addition, many savings and loan associations increased their holdings of Government securities in the mid- and late-1930s while waiting for a revival in the demand for residential financing.

During World War II, when the demand for residential financing declined sharply, savings and loan associations channeled almost all of their net savings inflows into Government securities. From 1941 through 1945, as assets rose from $6.0 billion to $8.7 billion, $2.4 billion went into this form of investment. By 1945, Government securities had risen to almost 30 per cent of the industry's portfolio.[39]

Investments since 1945

In 1945, 6,149 savings and loan associations held $7.4 billion in savings. By the end of 1964, although the number of organizations had increased to only 6,248, savings had risen to $101.8 billion. Savings and loan associations as a group had become the nation's largest holders of savings deposits. As a result of the prolonged post-World War II growth in the use of external financing for home construction and purchase as well as the increased safeguards in mortgage lending, residential mortgages generally provided the highest yields consistent with the levels of safety and liquidity necessary for the maintenance of thrift facilities. Thus, by continuing to concentrate in mortgage financing, savings and loan associations have been able to serve the interests of savers and homeowners at the same time. From 1945 through 1964 the net investments of savings and loan associations totaled $107.1 billion; more than 85 per cent of these were in residen-

[39] For a state-by-state record of the investment alternatives permitted savings and loan associations in 1925, see Clark and Chase, pp. 199–201; for the post-1945 period, see Kendall, *The Savings and Loan Business*, pp. 81–108, the United States Savings and Loan League, *Legal Bulletin*, July, 1964, and September, 1964, and Chart 2.

tial and commercial mortgages—primarily conventional—of which over 85 per cent were first liens on one- to four-family homes.

As a natural consequence of rapid growth, the desire for still further increases, and intensified competition for mortgages and savings deposits, savings and loan officials have made a considerable effort to have their industry's investment powers broadened. These officials feel that, if they are to continue competing effectively with other types of deposit institutions, they must have new outlets for funds as well as the added flexibility of being able to shift among a wider range of assets when market conditions change.

To the extent the investment powers of savings and loan associations have been widened, the changes have been predominantly in areas directly or closely related to home financing.[40] And in at least a few respects, the lending services of savings and loan associations have moved closer to those of mutual savings banks. For example, both may now invest up to 5 per cent of their assets in unsecured personal loans for the payment of college expenses and in any general obligations of states, political subdivisions, and federal agencies.

In addition, although the main difference between the investment opportunities of the two types of institutions is that mutual savings banks may purchase corporate securities while most savings and loan associations may not, even this distinction no longer exists everywhere. In New York, for instance, both types of state-chartered institutions are treated identically in this respect. State-chartered savings and loan associations are permitted to acquire any "securities in which investments are authorized to be made by mutual savings banks." [41]

Hoping to gain still broader investment opportunities, many savings and loan association officials—like many mutual savings bank officials—now argue that, because most homeowners need

[40] A complete list of the legislative changes relating to the investments of all federal- and state-chartered savings and loan associations appears in the United States Savings and Loan League, *Savings and Loan Annals* (Chicago: United States Savings and Loan League, 1954–64).

[41] *New York Banking Law*, Art. X, par. 379, sec. (5).

private transportation, permission to make automobile loans would be a logical extension of their industry's traditional interest in home financing. Furthermore, and for the same reason, many industry spokesmen propose that their organizations be allowed to finance the purchase of household appliances and furnishings. Bills to this effect are pending in many states as well as at the federal level, but as yet neither industry has been given specific permission to make loans of this type. As they continue to grow and as their investment interests continue to converge, savings and loan associations and mutual savings banks are likely to keep trying to move directly into consumer lending. Even now both groups make consumer loans indirectly by permitting homeowners to use the equity in their property as collateral for loans to finance such expenditures as education, travel, automobiles, boats, business ventures, stock purchases, or the consolidation of personal debts.

Thus, the basic functional similarities between savings and loan associations and mutual savings banks are evident: both accept savings that may be withdrawn at the discretion of the saver and invest the funds primarily in residential mortgages, with U.S. Government securities providing the major source of secondary liquidity.

3

Growth Rate Differences, 1945–1964

THE AVERAGE GROWTH RATES of all savings and loan associations as a group have been consistently higher than those of all mutual savings banks as a group each year from 1945 through 1964, even though the savings services of the two types of institutions have been fundamentally similar for many decades. Thus, the savings and loan association industry grew more rapidly not only when it was smaller than the mutual savings bank industry (from 1945 to 1953) but also after it had become equal to and greater than the size of all mutual savings banks together. Moreover, except for a very few years, the savings and loan association industry has also grown more rapidly than the mutual savings bank industry in every major region of the United States and also in every individual state in which both types of institutions provide savings facilities.

This chapter uses two measures of growth to document these observations: changes in the total savings held by each group and changes in the number of savings accounts and mutual savings bank deposits. With respect to total savings, growth rates are measured as annual gross changes (the year-end result of all additions—including interest accruals—less withdrawals) and as annual net changes (gross changes less interest accruals). The relevant data are presented for both industries at the national level, followed by a summary of the findings for all mutual savings bank states as a group, for each of the six states with the largest mutual savings bank deposits,[1] and for the remaining twelve mutual savings bank states together.[2] The trends at the national level are typical of those at all regional levels.[3] A concluding section compares the relative sizes of the two industries in 1945 and 1964 in each of the areas discussed.

NATIONWIDE COMPARISON OF SAVINGS GROWTH

Differences between the average annual growth rates of the savings and loan association and mutual savings bank industries during the twentieth century can be seen in Chart 3.[4] Except during part of the 1930s, savings and loan associations have grown more rapidly than mutual savings banks every year since 1905.

Looking only at the post-World War II period, it can be seen that savings were $7.4 billion in savings and loan associations in 1945 compared to $15.3 billion in mutual savings banks. During the next eight years, the former grew so much more rapidly that savings in the two groups were equal at $27 billion in 1954. Thereafter, the growth of savings and loan associations continued to be faster; by the end of 1964 savings accounts exceeded $101.8 billion, while mutual savings bank deposits totaled only $48.8 billion.

It might be expected that the savings and loan association industry would have grown more rapidly than the mutual savings bank industry during the years that the former was smaller.

[1] New York, Massachusetts, Connecticut, Pennsylvania, New Jersey, and Maryland.

[2] Maine, Rhode Island, New Hampshire, Vermont, Indiana, Washington, Wisconsin, Delaware, Ohio, Alaska, Minnesota, and Oregon.

[3] Similar trends are also apparent when the eighteen mutual savings bank states are divided into "high penetration" and "low penetration" states, with a "high penetration" state defined as one in which mutual savings banks hold at least half of the total savings deposits. These are New York, Massachusetts, Connecticut, New Hampshire, Rhode Island, and Maine. This division is discussed below.

[4] Gross and net savings from 1945 through 1964 in mutual savings banks and savings and loan associations in all of the regions discussed throughout this chapter appear in Appendix B.

CHART 3
Gross Savings in Mutual Savings Banks and Savings and
Loan Associations in the United States, 1900–1964

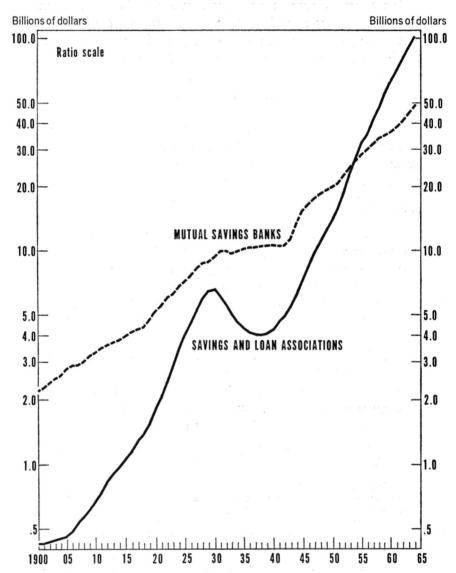

Sources: United States Savings and Loan League and National Association of
Mutual Savings Banks.

But if industry size were the only explanation for the relatively rapid growth of savings and loan associations, the spread between the annual growth rates of the two industries would have diminished as the size of the savings and loan associations approached the size of the mutual savings banks and would have reversed when the savings held by the former rose above savings held by the latter. But this was not the case. During the post-1945 period, the spread between the annual growth rates of the two groups continued to favor the savings and loan association industry even after its size exceeded that of the mutual savings bank industry.

CHART 4
Spreads Between the Average Annual Net Growth
Rates of Savings and Loan Associations and
Mutual Savings Banks in the
United States, 1946–1964 [a]

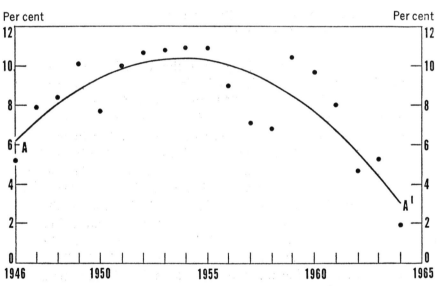

[a] Computed from data in Appendix B. AA′ is the best fitting third degree curve that can be drawn through the observations. Its equation, with its standard errors and coefficient of correlation, is:

$$SLA_{growth\ rate} - MSB_{growth\ rate} = 6.19 + 1.07t - .07t^2$$

$$(.20)\quad (.01)\qquad R^2 = .78$$

In comparing the growth of the two industries—with the ultimate purpose of trying to determine the reasons for the differences—it seems appropriate to exclude accrued interest payments which were based on different rates for each industry. Thus, Chart 4 measures differences between the annual net growth rates of savings and loan associations and mutual savings banks on the vertical axis, with time plotted on the horizontal axis. In net terms, savings and loan associations grew more rapidly than mutual savings banks throughout the period. Indeed, the spread was widest in the mid-1950s, when the two industries were approximately equal in size, and it continued to favor the savings and loan associations until the end of the period.

These data pose at least two questions for subsequent examination: What factors account for the difference in the annual average growth rates of the two industries? What has caused the spreads to be reduced in recent years?

NATIONWIDE COMPARISON OF GROWTH IN
THE NUMBER OF ACCOUNTS

In terms of the number of accounts, the disparity between the growth rates of the two industries is even more apparent. As indicated in Chart 5, from 1949 [5] through 1964, the number of accounts in savings and loan associations rose from 9.9 million to 38.9 million (290 per cent), while the number in mutual savings banks increased from 19.2 million to 22.2 million (less than 16 per cent). Over the same period, the number of accounts in savings and loan associations located in mutual savings bank states advanced from 5.5 million to 16.5 million (200 per cent). Moreover, the increase in the number of accounts in savings and loan associations exceeded the increase in mutual savings bank deposits annually from 1949 through 1964. This was true both nationwide and in all mutual savings bank states as a group, regardless of which industry was larger.

Unlike the situation for total savings, however, there was very little tendency for the growth rate spread between the two types

[5] This is the first year in which comparable data are available for both industries on a state-by-state basis.

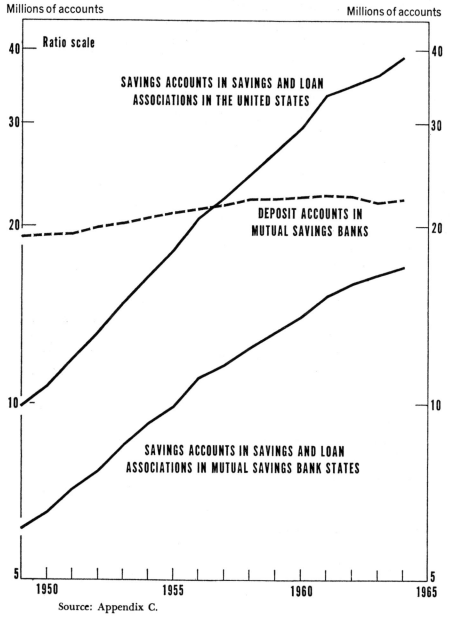

CHART 5

Number of Deposit and Savings Accounts in Mutual Savings
Banks and Savings and Loan Associations in the
United States and in Mutual Savings Bank
States, 1949–1964

Millions of accounts

Millions of accounts

Ratio scale

SAVINGS ACCOUNTS IN SAVINGS AND LOAN
ASSOCIATIONS IN THE UNITED STATES

DEPOSIT ACCOUNTS IN
MUTUAL SAVINGS BANKS

SAVINGS ACCOUNTS IN SAVINGS AND LOAN
ASSOCIATIONS IN MUTUAL SAVINGS BANK STATES

Source: Appendix C.

of institutions to narrow even after the number of accounts in savings and loan associations exceeded the number in mutual savings banks. This is shown on the two panels of Chart 6. Differences between the annual growth rates in the number of accounts held by savings and loan associations and mutual savings banks are measured on the vertical axis and time is plotted on the horizontal axis. Least squares lines, AA' and BB', are plotted through the observations, and although the lines are only roughly related to the observations, they at least suggest that the tendency for the growth rate spread to narrow was not very pronounced.[6]

GROWTH RATES IN MUTUAL SAVINGS BANK STATES

Unlike savings and loan associations, mutual savings banks are not located throughout the United States, and for many purposes comparisons between the two groups are of limited value at the national level. Mutual savings banks are chartered in only eighteen states, and approximately 82 per cent of their deposits are in New York, Massachusetts, and Connecticut. Charts 1 through 9 in Appendix A provide comparisons for the annual growth rates of the two types of institutions in all mutual savings bank states as a group, in each of the six states with the largest mutual savings bank deposits, in the twelve remaining mutual savings bank states together, in New York City, and in that part of New York State outside New York City. With only minor exceptions, the dominant trends in all of these regions are similar to those previously discussed.

In each case, savings and loan association growth rates exceeded those of mutual savings banks by considerable amounts over the entire 1945–64 period and in almost every individual

[6] Similar trends appear in the data for New York. From 1949 through 1964, the number of accounts in savings and loan associations rose 170 per cent, while the number in mutual savings banks grew only 23 per cent. See Appendix Chart 9.

The least squares line, of course, has the usual property that the sum of the squares of vertical deviations from the observations is smaller than the corresponding sum of the squares of deviations from any other line. Wilfred J. Dixon and Frank J. Massey, Jr., *Introduction to Statistical Analysis* (New York: McGraw-Hill, 1951), pp. 155–57.

CHART 6

Spreads Between the Annual Growth Rates of Savings and
Deposit Accounts in Savings and Loan Associations
and Mutual Savings Banks in the United States, 1949–1964

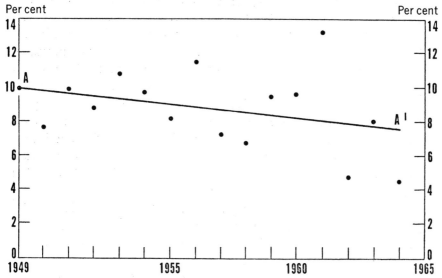

Spreads Between the Annual Growth Rates of Savings and
Deposit Accounts in Savings and Loan Associations
and Mutual Savings Banks in Mutual Savings Bank States, 1949–1964

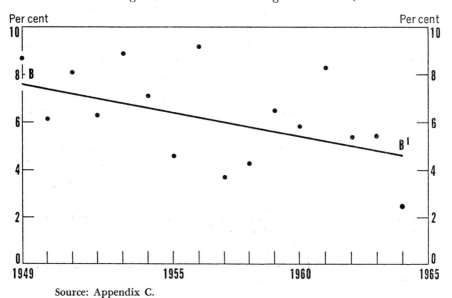

Source: Appendix C.

year as well. The major trends can be considered in three categories:

1. In all mutual savings bank states as a group, New York, Massachusetts, Connecticut, New York City, and that part of New York State outside New York City, the savings and loan association industry was consistently smaller than the mutual savings bank industry, and almost every year from 1945 through 1964 it grew consistently faster.[7] In all mutual savings bank states as a group and in New York State there was a slight tendency for the difference between the growth rates of the two groups to narrow over time; in Massachusetts and Connecticut, this tendency was considerably more pronounced. In New York City and in the portion of New York State outside of New York City the data show no specific trends.

2. In Pennsylvania, New Jersey, and Maryland, savings and loan associations started from a smaller size, grew more rapidly than mutual savings banks, became equal in size during the late 1940s or early 1950s, and then kept growing more rapidly than the mutual savings banks. The annual spread between the two sets of growth rates widened until the mid-1950s and started to narrow thereafter.[8]

3. In the twelve smallest mutual savings bank states as a group, the savings and loan association industry started from a larger size than the mutual savings bank industry and grew more rapidly every year of the post-1945 period except 1962 and 1964. Differences between the growth rates of the two industries widened until the mid-1950s and then started to narrow.[9]

Table 3 summarizes the effects of some of these trends. The amounts of savings held by mutual savings banks and savings and loan associations in 1945 and 1964 are recorded along with the size of the savings and loan associations as a proportion of the size of mutual savings bank savings in each region.[10] It can

[7] There was only one annual exception (1964) for New York, New York City, and the portion of New York State outside New York City and three exceptions in Massachusetts. See Appendix charts 1–5.

[8] See Appendix Chart 6.

[9] See Appendix charts 7 and 8.

[10] The years 1952 and 1964 are used for New York City and that part of New York State outside New York City.

be seen that, while in 1945 savings and loan associations in mutual savings bank states were only 29 per cent as large as mutual savings banks, the ratio in 1964 was 81 per cent. Similar changes appear in each of the other categories. The percentage change in the amount of savings held by each group over the twenty-year period is in the two columns at the far right. In each case, the over-all growth rate for savings and loan associations is considerably greater than the over-all growth rate for mutual savings banks. In mutual savings bank states, for example, savings and loan associations grew by 798 per cent while mutual savings bank growth was only 219 per cent.[11] It is interesting to note, moreover, that in all mutual savings bank states as a group, savings and loan associations realized $1.6 billion more than mutual savings banks in savings growth over the period. Beginning with $4.4 billion, savings and loan associations grew by $35.1 billion, while mutual savings banks, starting with $15.3 billion, realized only $33.5 billion in additional deposits. In three out of the last four years of the period, savings and loan association growth also exceeded mutual savings bank growth in absolute as well as in percentage terms.

When a distinction is made between high penetration states (in which mutual savings banks hold over half of the total savings deposits) and low penetration states (in which mutual savings banks hold less than half of the total savings deposits), rather than according to the volume of deposits, similar trends appear.[12] In New Hampshire, Rhode Island, and Maine, savings and loan association growth rates exceeded mutual savings bank growth rates almost every year from 1945 through 1964 (with only one exception in Maine and four in Rhode Island), although there has been a marked tendency for the savings and loan

11 While one might expect the savings and loan associations to grow more rapidly than the mutual savings banks simply because of their smaller size, the data and discussion on pp. 71–74 indicate that throughout the post-World War II period there has been no tendency for smaller savings and loan associations or mutual savings banks to grow more rapidly than larger ones.

12 New York, Massachusetts, and Connecticut are high penetration and high volume states; New Hampshire, Rhode Island, and Maine are the other high penetration states; Pennsylvania, New Jersey, and Maryland are high volume, but not high penetration, states.

TABLE 3

Savings in Mutual Savings Banks and Savings and Loan Associations in Selected Regions, 1945 and 1964

(In billions of dollars)

Region	1945			1964			Percentage Change 1945–64	
	MSB	SLA	SLA ÷ MSB	MSB	SLA	SLA ÷ MSB	MSB	SLA
All mutual savings bank states	$15.3	$4.4	.29	$48.8	$ 39.5	.81	219	798
New York	8.3	0.6	.07	28.3	6.5	.23	241	983
Massachusetts	2.9	0.8	.28	7.9	2.7	.34	172	238
Connecticut	1.1	0.1	.09	3.5	0.9	.26	218	800
Pennsylvania	0.9	0.6	.67	3.0	4.7	1.57	233	683
New Jersey	0.4	0.3	.75	1.9	3.8	2.00	375	1,167
Maryland	0.4	0.2	.50	0.7	1.8	2.57	75	800
Twelve remaining mutual savings bank states	1.4	2.1	1.50	3.7	19.2	5.19	164	814
United States	15.3	7.4	.48	48.8	101.8	2.09	219	1,276
		1952			**1964**		**1952–64**	
New York City	$10.6	$0.8	.08	$22.4	$ 3.5	.16	111	338
New York State outside of New York City	2.7	0.8	.30	6.0	3.1	.52	122	288

Source: Appendix B.

association growth rate advantage to narrow in recent years. In these states—unlike Pennsylvania, New Jersey, and Maryland— savings and loan associations as a group were much smaller than mutual savings banks as a group throughout the entire period, thus providing three examples of situations in which the former grew more rapidly even though the latter were apparently more strongly established.

TABLE 4

Percentage of Total Savings in Mutual Savings Banks, Savings and Loan Associations, and Commercial Banks, Selected Regions, 1945 and 1964 [a]

Region	1945				1964			
	Total	MSB	SLA	CB	Total	MSB	SLA	CB
New York	100.0	69.3	2.6	27.7	100.0	56.8	13.2	30.0
Massachusetts	100.0	76.4	4.3	19.4	100.0	67.2	21.9	10.9
Connecticut	100.0	73.5	4.0	22.4	100.0	66.5	17.1	16.4
Pennsylvania	100.0	25.8	5.9	68.4	100.0	19.2	31.5	49.3
New Jersey	100.0	18.8	1.0	80.2	100.0	18.6	37.9	43.5
Maryland	100.0	42.9	9.1	48.0	100.0	22.8	41.7	35.5
Twelve remaining mutual savings bank states	100.0	12.5	19.6	67.9	100.0	10.1	47.3	42.6
All mutual savings bank states	100.0	47.8	5.4	46.8	100.0	36.8	28.5	34.7
United States	100.0	14.1	29.6	56.3	100.0	18.4	38.8	42.8

[a] Calculated from data in Appendix B and from the Federal Deposit Insurance Corporation, *Annual Reports*. Figures for commercial banks include time as well as savings deposits.

Table 4 shows what the different growth rates from 1945 through 1964 mean in terms of changes in the relative importance of savings and loan associations and mutual savings banks among deposit-receiving industries generally. Inasmuch as these two groups and commercial banks held about 96 per cent of all savings and time deposits throughout the post-1945 period, data for the latter are included for purposes of comparison.

In each of the six states with the largest mutual savings bank deposits, in the twelve remaining mutual savings bank states as a group, and in all mutual savings bank states combined, the relative share of savings and loan associations increased substantially, while the relative importance of mutual savings banks declined. In each of the six largest states, for example, the share of mutual savings banks fell—from 0.2 percentage point in New Jersey to 20.1 percentage points in Maryland—while the share of savings and loan associations rose from 10.6 percentage points in New York to 36.9 percentage points in New Jersey. In all mutual savings bank states as a group, the share of savings and loan associations advanced by 23.1 percentage points, while that of mutual savings banks declined by 9.0 percentage points. In the entire United States, although both industries improved their positions at the expense of commercial banks, the increases were 9.2 percentage points for savings and loan associations and only 4.3 percentage points for mutual savings banks.

Thus, as would be expected, deterioration of the mutual savings banks' position relative to that of savings and loan associations is just as apparent in terms of changes in the comparative importance of the two groups among deposit industries generally as it is with respect to their relative growth rates.

4

Location as a Fundamental Factor in Growth Rate Differences

DESPITE THEIR STRUCTURAL and functional similarities, an underlying reason for the persistently higher growth rates of savings and loan associations than of mutual savings banks is that the former have been located predominantly in more rapidly growing regions during a period when savings deposit growth was closely related to local changes in population and income. In every state served by the two types of institutions, mutual savings banks have been heavily concentrated in major metropolitan centers—areas with declining populations and only moderately rising per capita incomes—while savings and loan associations have been widely dispersed throughout the surrounding suburban and other nonurban regions where population and per capita income have been rising more rapidly. Moreover, many savings and loan associations have been located in rapidly growing states that have no provisions for chartering mutual savings banks.

The analysis in this chapter and the next three tests the premise that from 1945 through 1964 almost all individuals held their savings accounts in organizations located close to their homes, jobs, or shopping districts, even when higher interest payments were available from more distant institutions and even when there appeared to be differences in the safety and liquidity of the various institutions. These findings are then related to locational differences and finally to growth rate differences between savings and loan associations and mutual savings banks.[1]

SERVICE DIFFERENTIATION

Similarity among institutions depends, of course, entirely on how broadly or how narrowly the basic characteristics are defined. In this respect, financial organizations are no different from retail stores, professional services, or any other organization or individual with a product or service to market.[2]

The major ways that most mutual savings banks and savings and loan associations differentiate their savings services can be expressed in terms of office location, interest payments, safety, and liquidity[3] The principal effects of lending operations on the growth of financial intermediaries are transmitted to savers through one or more of these mechanisms. Thus, the following

[1] Precise quantification of the relevant relationships between location, interest rates, attitudes toward safety and liquidity, and relative growth rates involves problems that are outside the scope of this study. By combining simple correlation techniques with a primarily descriptive method, however, the importance of certain growth determinants can be made apparent, whereas they previously have been largely ignored in favor of the more quantifiable variables.

[2] The classic description of product and service differentiation within a competitive framework appears in Edward Chamberlin, *The Theory of Monopolistic Competition* (Cambridge, Mass.: Harvard University Press, 1934). See especially pp. 56–57. An application of these concepts to banking appears in Lester V. Chandler, "Monopolistic Elements in Commercial Banking," *Journal of Political Economy*, XLVI (February, 1938), 1–22.

[3] The effect of advertising expenditures is included in the discussion of interest payments. The importance of auxiliary savings services and the conveniences of "one-stop" commercial banking are examined in chapter 6. Other aspects of service differentiation, such as architectural elegance, quality of personnel, or special office hours—although they may be important in specific cases—are not sufficiently significant to warrant separate treatment. In addition, to the extent that institutions receive higher yields by purchasing conventional mortgages directly, rather than purchasing FHA and VA mortgages through an intermediary, and to the extent that mortgagees often save with organizations from which they get their loans, mutual savings banks in city centers have been in a poor position to participate in the growth generated by the owner-occupied housing boom of the post–World War II period. Because of the scarcity of relevant data, these effects are not discussed in detail in this chapter; but to the degree that they influence savings growth, the savings and loan associations are favored over mutual savings banks.

analysis concentrates almost entirely on differences among savings services.

RELATION BETWEEN THE SIZE OF INDIVIDUAL INSTITUTIONS AND INDUSTRY GROWTH RATES

Because industry growth rates result from changes in the size of individual institutions, it might be argued that the underlying reason for the spread of post-1945 growth rates between savings and loan associations and mutual savings banks is that the average savings and loan association started each year from a smaller size than the average mutual savings bank (see Table 5). Yet, the idea that smaller financial intermediaries necessarily grow more rapidly than larger ones is actually contrary to post-1945 experience.

TABLE 5

Average Assets in Savings and Loan Associations
and Mutual Savings Banks, Selected Years
(*In millions of dollars*)

	Savings and Loan Associations	Mutual Savings Banks
1945	1.4	32.0
1950	2.8	42.4
1955	6.2	59.4
1960	11.4	78.8
1964	19.2	107.2

Source: National Association of Mutual Savings Banks, *National Fact Book, 1965*, p. 5.

To demonstrate this, Table 6 groups mutual savings banks and savings and loan associations according to size. The percentage of each industry's assets held in various categories is recorded for selected years. It can be seen that among mutual savings banks there was a slight tendency for larger organizations to grow *more rapidly* than smaller ones, while growth rates among savings and loan associations were relatively the same at all levels. The share of the 100 largest mutual savings banks, for

TABLE 6

Percentage of Industry Assets in Mutual Savings Banks and
Savings and Loan Associations, Selected Years

		Mutual Savings Banks				
		1945	*1950*	*1955*	*1960*	*1964*
Largest	10	22.6	24.6	24.0	23.9	23.6
	20	34.9	36.9	36.5	36.5	36.0
	30	43.3	45.5	45.6	45.7	45.9
	40	49.6	52.0	52.3	52.5	52.1
	50	54.5	56.9	57.3	57.6	57.3
	60	58.7	60.9	61.6	62.0	61.8
	70	62.4	64.5	65.3	65.8	65.6
	80	65.5	67.6	68.5	68.9	68.7
	90	68.2	70.2	71.1	71.6	71.4
	100	70.7	72.6	73.4	74.0	73.8
	200	86.2	86.0	86.6	87.4	86.8
	300	92.5	92.1	92.6	93.4	93.1
	400	96.2	96.4	96.3	96.6	96.8
Remainder		3.8	3.6	3.7	3.4	3.2

		Savings and Loan Associations				
Largest	10	5.6	4.9	5.0	6.0	5.6
	20	9.4	8.1	8.6	9.6	9.7
	30	12.4	10.6	11.1	12.3	12.3
	40	14.9	12.8	13.1	14.6	14.4
	50	17.0	14.6	15.3	16.5	16.5
	60	18.8	16.3	16.9	18.2	18.3
	70	20.6	17.9	18.5	19.9	20.0
	80	22.1	20.7	20.0	21.4	21.5
	90	23.6	22.1	21.4	22.7	22.8
	100	25.1	23.3	22.6	24.0	24.2
	150	30.3	30.2	28.2	28.0	29.9
	200	n.a.	35.9	32.8	33.1	34.6
	300	n.a.	n.a.	40.1	41.6	41.9
Remainder		n.a.	n.a.	59.9	58.4	58.1

Source: Mutual savings bank figures for 1945 are from National Association of Mutual Savings Banks, *This Month's Work*, February, 1949, p. 14. Other data are from selected issues of the *American Banker* and from the National Association of Mutual Savings Banks.
n.a. = Not available.

example, rose from 70.7 per cent in 1945 to 73.8 per cent in 1964, while the share held by the largest 100 savings and loan associations declined by only nine tenths of 1 per cent over the same period.

TABLE 7

Distribution of Savings and Loan Associations and
Mutual Savings Banks by Asset Size, 1960
(*In millions of dollars*)

	Total	*Less than* $5.0	$5.0– 9.9	$10.0– 49.9	$50.0– 99.9	$100.0 and over
Savings and loan associations [a]	4,694	2,049	968	1,403	185	89
Mutual savings banks	515	34	67	226	95	93

Sources: U.S. Congress, House of Representatives, *Comparative Regulations of Financial Institutions*, 88th Cong., 1st Sess., 1963, pp. 69, 106; National Association of Mutual Savings Banks.

[a] Savings and loan associations here are Federal Home Loan Bank System members only.

Table 7 provides information for an interindustry comparison. All mutual savings banks and all savings and loan associations in the Federal Home Loan Bank System in 1960 are grouped into five categories by asset size. Although the average, median, and mode for mutual savings banks were all above those for savings and loan associations, there was a considerable number of both types of institutions within each asset category.

If growth rate differences among savings and loan associations and mutual savings banks were primarily a function of the relative size of individual institutions, the 250 largest savings and loan associations (all of which had assets over $50 million) would not have been expected to grow more rapidly than the 250 smallest mutual savings banks (all of which had assets under $50 million). Yet, with growth rates among savings and loan associations consistently higher than those of mutual savings banks and with growth rates among the two industries much the same at all size levels, it appears that the larger savings and loan associations *were* growing more rapidly than smaller mutual savings banks during the 1945–64 period. Thus, although the relative size of individual institutions may have been a factor influencing the growth rates of the two industries, it was clearly not the overriding determinant.

GEOGRAPHIC ORIGINS OF THE SAVERS

All available information indicates that during the post-1945 period individuals with savings accounts in either mutual savings banks or savings and loan associations demonstrated an overwhelming preference for doing business with organizations located close to their homes, jobs, or shopping districts. In most cases, it appears that the real and imagined costs of dealing with distant organizations more than offset the advantages.[4]

Two important studies help document these observations: the first was made in 1958, of the major types of deposit institutions in New York,[5] the second in 1959, of the majority of savings and loan associations in California.[6] In the first case, it was found that in virtually all non-New York City mutual savings banks and savings and loan associations more than 80 per cent of the savers lived within the city, town, or "immediate environs"—the area within the customary commuting distance—in which the organization was located. For more than three quarters of the institutions, the figure was over 90 per cent; and, of course, at least part (and possibly all) of the remainder lived in the immediately surrounding rural areas. When the amount deposited—rather than the number of depositors—was considered, similar proportions were reported.[7] Complementary sur-

[4] In many cases there are no tangible costs in dealing with distant institutions. In these instances, intangible costs—such as a sense of anxiety or inconvenience—appear to be large indeed. Limited knowledge concerning available alternatives, especially among savers with small accounts, is also an important factor creating an imperfect market.

[5] New York State Banking Department, *Postwar Banking Developments in New York State* (New York: New York State Banking Department, 1958).

[6] Stanford Research Institute, "California Savings and Loan Associations" (Pasadena, Calif.: Stanford Research Institute, 1959).

[7] New York State Banking Department, pp. 38–41.

veys indicate that virtually all individuals saving with mutual savings banks and savings and loan associations in New York City lived or worked in one of the five boroughs or surrounding suburban and rural regions.

However, the fact that mutual savings banks and savings and loan associations in New York received most of their deposits from within a comparatively small area surrounding each organization does not eliminate the possibility that New York residents might have been sending savings to deposit institutions in other states. In 1958, or in any other post-1945 year, if a New Yorker had been induced to hold a savings deposit in any other state, he probably would have selected one of the California savings and loan associations that during this period were offering higher interest rates than deposit-receiving institutions anywhere else in the nation. Therefore, as an indication of whether or not there was a substantial flow of funds from New York into deposit institutions in other states, the following paragraphs refer to the geographic origins of people with accounts in California savings and loan associations.

In 1959, when the Stanford Research Institute surveyed 413 California savings and loan associations—with about half of the assets in all California savings and loan associations that year—it was found that 40 per cent of the savers lived less than two miles from the organization with which they did business and that 95 per cent lived within a radius of less than 25 miles.[8] Undoubtedly, at least a part of the remaining 5 per cent lived not much further than 25 miles away. In terms of total deposits the figures are similar. Thus, in 1959, only a very small portion of the California savers could have been from New York—and even that portion could have been attracted from either mutual savings banks or savings and loan associations, thereby suggesting no reason why savings and loan associations were growing constantly faster than mutual savings banks *within* New York State.

Subsequent studies suggest that out-of-state savings flows into California savings and loan associations increased somewhat in

[8] Stanford Research Institute, pp. viii, 15–16.

the years immediately following the Stanford Research Institute study, reaching about 8 per cent of the total growth of the California savings and loan associations from 1960 through 1962.[9] These savings went primarily into publically owned, capital stock savings and loan associations, the first of which was formed in December, 1959. But further evidence indicates that this flow of out-of-state savings has slowed down substantially since 1962 and may even have been reversed as interest payment differentials between East- and West-coast institutions narrowed to less than one percentage point. In any case, savings flows into capital stock organizations in California cannot explain the growth rate differences between savings and loan associations and mutual savings banks prior to 1959; nor can they explain growth rate differences that persisted from 1959 through 1964 between savings and loan associations and mutual savings banks *within* New York and within each of the other mutual savings bank states as well.

Literally hundreds of smaller studies complement the findings of the New York State Banking Department and the Stanford Research Institute. Individual mutual savings banks and savings and loan associations are continually making surveys of population and income so that new offices can be located where they are likely to attract the most savings. The assumption underlying the opening of any new office is that it will attract its funds primarily from local savers.

Furthermore, as the following quotation from *The New York Times* indicates, the importance of location is not a matter of states or miles, but frequently of blocks or of being near an appropriate subway stop. The paper reports:

World of Finance Finds Avenue M—For twenty-seven years the bustling, middle-class shopping district that straddles the Avenue M station of the BMT had no bank or savings institution of its own . . . Tradesmen and housewives who wanted to borrow money or make a deposit had to trek or drive four long blocks to Kings Highway or

9 For example, see Leo Grebler and Eugene F. Brigham, *Savings and Mortgage Markets in California* (Pasadena, Calif.: California Savings and Loan League, 1963), pp. 83–86.

three long blocks to Avenue J. . . . All that is changing rapidly. What makes a Brooklyn neighborhood that for twenty-seven years had no financial establishment of any kind suddenly attractive enough to bring in two thrift institutions and a commercial bank? Prosperity and population, primarily. And secondarily, the keen competition among New York City's banks.[10]

Admittedly, these observations are very general. They do not indicate why most people prefer to save near their homes or places of business or what interest payment spread or type of service differentiation would have been necessary to overcome this preference. Moreover, they say nothing about reasons for choosing between two closely located institutions or about choices involving the convenience of location versus the convenience of one-stop banking. Neither do they explain why some savers travel or send money to distant deposit institutions.

But these and many other studies do indicate that, at the end of a period in which the average annual growth rates of savings and loan associations had exceeded those of mutual savings banks for more than two decades, almost all savers doing business with these institutions maintained accounts in organizations comparatively close to where they lived, worked, or shopped. Thus, to analyze the reasons for the different growth rates of these industries, an examination must be made of the number of locations maintained by each industry and of the relevant changes within each area being served.

OFFICE EXPANSION

Contrary to what might be expected, considering the annual spread between the average growth rates of savings and loan associations and mutual savings banks, the rate of total office growth in the 1945-64 period was greater for mutual savings banks than for savings and loan associations. Table 8 indicates a gain of 81 per cent in mutual savings bank offices and only 50 per cent for savings and loan associations and 25 per cent for savings and loan associations in mutual savings bank states.

10 *The New York Times,* December 28, 1963, p. 27.

TABLE 8
Increases in Total Offices (Main Plus Branch) of
Savings and Loan Associations and Mutual Savings Banks
in Selected Regions, 1945–1964 [a]

	All SLA	All MSB	SLA in MSB States	New York		Massa-chusetts		Con-necticut	
				SLA	MSB	SLA	MSB	SLA	MSB
Absolute gain	3,051	547	867	168	166	34	114	28	102
Percentage gain	50	81	25	68	87	57	66	58	142

Sources: United States Savings and Loan League, *Savings and Loan Annals* and National Association of Mutual Savings Banks, *National Fact Book.*

[a] Although figures are not available for the number of savings and loan association branches prior to 1953, indications are that there were very few. For computing changes in the total number of savings and loan association offices, it is assumed that there were no branches in 1945 and the number of institutions is used as the divisor. Thus, increases for savings and loan associations may have a slight upward bias.

The rate of office expansion was also greater for mutual savings banks in New York (where the number of new offices was about the same for both industries), in Massachusetts and Connecticut (where the number of new mutual savings bank offices exceeded by considerable amounts the number of new savings and loan association offices), and in almost all other mutual savings bank states as well. Thus, in all regions the interesting point is that savings and loan associations grew more rapidly than mutual savings banks in almost every year of the post-1945 period even though the rate of increase of mutual savings bank offices exceeded that of savings and loan associations. An explanation must be found for this difference.

RELATION BETWEEN CHANGES IN TOTAL PERSONAL INCOME
AND SAVINGS GROWTH

For the period 1950–64 there are direct and highly significant statistical relationships on a state-by-state basis between changes in total personal income and the growth of all deposit-receiving institutions as a group, with substantial differences with respect to savings and loan associations and commercial banks on the one hand and mutual savings banks on the other hand.

To demonstrate this, the following analysis first considers data for thirty-one nonmutual savings bank states (excluding Hawaii) and then for seventeen mutual savings bank states (excluding Alaska). It is believed that each state constitutes a large enough area and contains a large enough number of deposit institutions to smooth out local peculiarities in savings habits and that the number of observations are sufficient to indicate certain dominant relationships. Savings and loan associations, mutual savings banks, and commercial banks are used to represent all deposit-receiving institutions inasmuch as they hold over 96 per cent of all savings deposits and accounts.[11] Total personal income is used as a measure of income because it is the only series for which data or a reasonable proxy is available for comparisons by state, by city, and in selected nonurban regions. Finally, 1950 through 1964 is used rather than the entire post-1945 period to eliminate the years immediately following World War II when dissavings were unusually high. A statistical procedure—rank correlation—is used to examine the extent of the relationship between changes in total personal income and savings deposit growth.[12]

[11] Time and savings deposits are used for commercial banks.

[12] With this procedure, the states are first ranked from high to low on the basis of the percentage rates at which their total personal income increased from 1950 through 1964; they are then ranked according to the rates at which their savings deposits increased during the same period. The coefficients of rank correlation indicate the extent of agreement between the two rankings, with a value of $+1$ indicating perfect agreement and a value of -1 indicating that the two rankings are exactly the opposite of each other. Of course, most coefficients fall between these limits. In each case a test can be applied to see if the coefficient is greater than what would be expected if the two sets of rankings were independent, i.e., if there were no significant relationship between them. The higher the coefficient, the greater the confidence in its significance.

In this case—with the distribution of the two sets of data strongly skewed—the use of rank correlation analysis is more appropriate than simple correlation or regression analysis. While the latter assumes that the variables are normally distributed, the former makes no assumptions about the distribution of the variables. The coefficient of rank correlation is derived with the formula $r = \dfrac{1 - 6\Sigma d^2}{N(N^2 - 1)}$. See Helen M. Walker and Joseph Lev, *Statistical Inference* (New York: Henry Holt, 1953), p. 278.

The coefficients of rank correlation in Table 9 indicate relationships for the thirty-one nonmutual savings bank states that are all direct and highly significant; that is, savings deposits in each type of institution grew at the most rapid percentage rate in the states where increases in total personal income were most rapid, and vice versa. The relationship is highest, + .89, when the growth of both types of institutions is combined.

TABLE 9

Coefficients of Rank Correlation Between State-by-State Rates of Change in Total Personal Income and Rates of Savings Deposit Growth, Selected Regions, 1950–1964

31 Nonmutual Savings Bank States

(1) Savings in savings and loan associations	+ .65
(2) Time and savings deposits in commercial banks	+ .83
(3) (1) + (2)	+ .89

17 Mutual Savings Bank States

(1) Savings in savings and loan associations	+ .18
(2) Time and savings deposits in commercial banks	+ .29
(3) Deposits in mutual savings banks	− .21
(4) (1) + (2) + (3)	+ .68

Sources: Selected issues of the United States Savings and Loan League, *Savings and Loan Annals;* National Association of Mutual Savings Banks, *National Fact Book;* Federal Deposit Insurance Corporation, *Annual Report;* and the U.S. Department of Commerce, *Statistical Abstract.*

In the seventeen mutual savings bank states, however, the relationships are quite different. The growth rates of savings and loan associations and commercial banks, considered separately, are altered to the point where they are no longer significantly related to state-by-state changes in total personal income. And when the growth rates of mutual savings banks in the seventeen states are related to the rates of increase in total personal income, the association is also not significant; in fact, the relationship is inverse, suggesting that on a statewide basis mutual savings bank growth is least rapid where the growth of total personal income is most rapid. However, the savings growth of all institutions combined is significantly related to statewide changes in total personal income, as it is in the nonmutual savings bank states.

Thus, unlike the data for nonmutual savings bank states, it appears that statewide changes in total personal income in mutual savings bank states do not explain the different growth rate patterns of each industry separately. Perhaps this is because mutual savings bank competition—with the mutual savings bank industry large in some states and small in others—distorts the typical statewide relationships. Or perhaps within each mutual savings bank state there are important differences in the locations of the different types of institutions, making it inappropriate to expect high correlations between *statewide* changes in total personal income and growth. Moreover, there may be substantial differences in population and income changes within the different areas being served. These possibilities can be tested by an examination of the locations of mutual savings banks and savings and loan associations within the mutual savings bank states.[13]

LOCATIONS IN NEW YORK STATE

Data on the following pages indicate that there are indeed important differences in the locations of mutual savings banks and

[13] The possibility that locational differences may be significant in distorting the more typical relationship between statewide changes in total personal income and savings growth is suggested even more clearly by the relationships between *absolute* increases in total personal income and *absolute* savings deposit growth. The following data indicate that while the savings deposit growth of savings and loan associations and commercial banks is very closely related to statewide increases in total personal income, mutual savings bank growth is not.

Coefficients of Rank Correlation Between Changes in Total
Personal Income and Changes in Savings Deposits
in Selected Institutions in 17 Mutual
Savings Banks States, 1950–1964

(1) Savings in savings and loan associations	+ .92
(2) Time and savings deposits in commercial banks	+ .95
(3) Deposits in mutual savings banks	+ .18
(4) (1) + (2) + (3)	+ .97

Sources: See Table 9.

savings and loan associations within each state, with mutual savings banks far more heavily concentrated in major metropolitan centers. The figures for New York are discussed in some detail and the relevant material is then summarized for each of the other large mutual savings bank states and the twelve smallest mutual savings bank states as a group.

The comparison in New York is particularly revealing inasmuch as the number of offices opened by each type of institution from 1945 through 1964 was closer than in any other mutual savings bank state. And, as subsequent chapters demonstrate, the average interest payments offered by the two industries, as well as attitudes toward the safety and liquidity of their savings accounts, have been fundamentally similar since at least the mid-1950s. Despite these likenesses, savings and loan associations in that state have grown more rapidly than mutual savings banks in every post-1945 year except 1964, with the spread between their growth rates averaging 6.0 per cent annually over the entire period.

Table 10 divides all New York savings and loan association and mutual savings bank offices (main, branch, and total) into two categories—urban and nonurban—for 1950, 1959, and 1964.[14] Changes in the number of offices in each category are recorded for 1950–59, 1959–64, and 1950–64.

In 1950, 156 out of 289 (54 per cent) of the savings and loan association offices were in nonurban locations. Over the fifteen-year period, 55 additional offices were opened in nonurban areas as opposed to only 44 in urban regions.

For mutual savings banks, the figures are significantly different. In 1950, *more than three times* as many mutual savings bank offices were in urban as compared with nonurban regions (183 versus 52). Furthermore, from 1950 through 1964, 55 new

[14] The term "urban" refers to all areas within the city limits of New York City (all boroughs), Albany, Binghamton, Utica-Rome, Syracuse, Rochester, and Buffalo. These are the seven largest cities in New York. "Nonurban" refers to the rest of the state. The year 1959 is the last year preceding passage of the Omnibus Banking Act, which liberalized suburban branching opportunities for mutual savings banks.

TABLE 10

Locations of Savings and Loan Association and Mutual Savings Bank Offices
in New York, 1950, 1959, and 1964

SAVINGS AND LOAN ASSOCIATIONS

	1950			Change, 1950–59			1959			Change, 1959–64			1964			Change, 1950–64		
	Main	Branch	Total	Main	Branch	Total	Main	Branch	Total	Main	Branch	Total	Main	Branch	Total	Main	Branch	Total
Urban [a]	83	50	133	4	23	27	87	73	160	2	15	17	89	88	177	6	38	44
Nonurban	128	28	156	0	20	20	128	48	176	9	26	35	137	74	211	9	46	55
Total	211	78	289	4	43	47	215	121	336	11	41	52	226	162	388	15	84	99

MUTUAL SAVINGS BANKS

	1950			Change, 1950–59			1959			Change, 1959–64			1964			Change, 1950–64		
	Main	Branch	Total	Main	Branch	Total	Main	Branch	Total	Main	Branch	Total	Main	Branch	Total	Main	Branch	Total
Urban	81	102	183	−1	32	31	80	134	214	−1	25	24	78	160	238	−3	58	55
Nonurban	49	3	52	−1	9	8	48	12	60	−1	40	39	47	53	100	−2	50	47
Total	130	105	235	−2	41	39	128	146	274	−2	65	63	125	213	338	−5	108	102

Sources: New York State Banking Department, *Report of the Superintendent of Banks, State of New York* (New York: New York State Banking Department, 1951, 1960, 1965), and the Federal Home Loan Bank of New York.

[a] "Urban" and "nonurban" are defined in footnote 14, p. 82.

offices were opened in urban areas as opposed to only 47 in nonurban regions.[15]

Thus, throughout the fifteen-year span, most savings and loan association offices were in suburban and other nonurban areas, while mutual savings bank offices were predominantly in the largest cities of the state. Moreover, the number and the proportion of additional savings and loan association offices opened in nonurban regions was greater than the number and the proportion for mutual savings banks.

Unfortunately for the purposes of ascertaining the proportion of each industry's assets held in these urban and nonurban offices, a breakdown of assets by main and branch offices is not available. Figures are available on an institution-by-institution basis, however, and the relevant data appear in Table 11.

In 1964, 40 per cent of the savings and loan association offices were in urban locations. These held 61 per cent of that industry's New York assets. At the same time, 63 per cent of the mutual savings bank offices, holding *93 per cent* of all mutual savings bank assets in the state, were in urban regions. Thus, in terms of assets as well as offices, a much larger proportion of mutual savings banks than savings and loan associations was located in the state's major urban regions. It is now important to ascertain whether or not there have been any basic differences in changes in total personal income between the urban and nonurban regions of New York. Table 12 indicates that there have been.

Using population and median family income to approximate

15 Comparing mutual savings bank data before and after restrictions on branch banking were liberalized by the Omnibus Banking Act of 1960, it is seen that whereas mutual savings banks opened 32 new branch offices in urban locations from 1950 through 1959, compared to only 9 in nonurban regions, the figures were 25 and 40 for 1959 through 1964, respectively. Moreover, the growth rates of mutual savings banks in New York State as a whole would have been substantially slower since 1960 were it not for deposit increases in the suburban branches opened pursuant to the Omnibus Banking Act. For details on the growth of these offices, see Savings Bank Association of New York State, "The Savings Banks of New York State: Their Need to Grow and Expand in the Interests and Economy of the State" (New York: Savings Bank Association of New York State, 1964). For more recent data, see Savings Bank Association of New York State, *Savings Bank Fact Book, 1967* (New York: Savings Bank Association of New York State, 1967).

TABLE 11

Number and Assets of Urban and Nonurban Mutual Savings Banks and Savings and Loan Associations in New York in 1964 [a]

(Assets in millions of dollars)

(1) Number		(2) Number in Urban Regions		(3) (2) ÷ (1)		(4) Total Assets		(5) Assets in Urban Regions		(6) (4) ÷ (5)	
SLA	*MSB*	*SLA*	*MSB*	*SLA*	*MSB*	*SLA*	*MSB*	*SLA*	*MSB*	*SLA*	*MSB*
225	125	90	78	40%	62%	$7,870	$31,455	$4,495	$29,253	61%	93%

[a] Calculated from data in Table 10, National Association of Mutual Savings Banks, *Directory and Guide, 1965–66* (New York: National Association of Mutual Savings Banks, 1965), and T. K. Sanderson Organization, *Directory of American Savings and Loan Associations, 1965–66* (Baltimore: T. K. Sanderson Organization, 1965). Definitions of "urban" and "nonurban" appear in footnote 14, p. 82.

total personal income,[16] Table 12 records the relevant decennial census figures for 1950 and 1960 for each of the seven cities comprising the urban regions of the state (as defined in footnote 14, page 82), for the surrounding suburban areas (the portion of each standard metropolitan statistical area outside the city center), and for the state as a whole.[17]

In every case—and this is typical of almost all major cities in the United States—the population of the city center declined during the period being examined. Decreases ranged from 1.1 per cent in the Utica-Rome complex to 8.2 per cent in Buffalo. At the same time—as in almost all suburban areas throughout the nation—population rose sharply in that portion of every standard metropolitan statistical area outside the central city. Advances ranged from 26.7 per cent for the Utica-Rome area to 75.0 per cent for New York City.

The number of people in the seven urban areas where most mutual savings banks were located declined by 3.1 per cent, while the population in the nonurban regions, where most of the savings and loan association offices were located, grew by 46.1 per cent. Population in the state as a whole advanced by 14.2 per cent.

Data for median family income are not available for that portion of the standard metropolitan statistical area outside of each city center. Therefore, Table 12 compares the figures for each city with those for its *entire* statistical area. This undoubtedly *understates* by considerable amounts the disparities between income changes in the cities and income changes in the respective

16 Figures for average per capita income are not available for the years and regions discussed.

17 Standard metropolitan statistical areas are essentially the cities plus their suburban regions. According to the Bureau of the Census, "The definition of an individual SMSA involves two considerations: first, a city or cities of specified population to constitute the central city and to identify the county in which it is located as the central county; and, second, economic and social relationships with contiguous areas which are metropolitan in character, so that the periphery of the specified metropolitan area may be determined. SMSA's may cross state lines." U.S. Bureau of the Census, Department of Commerce, *Census of Population, 1960: United States Summary* (Washington, D.C.: Government Printing Office, 1962), p. ix.

TABLE 12

Population and Median Family Income in Selected Areas
of New York, 1950, 1960, and 1950–1960

	Population (in thousands)		Percent- age Change	Median Family Income (in dollars)		Percent- age Change
	1950	*1960*	*1950–60*	*1950*	*1960*	*1950–60*
New York City a	7,893	7,781	− 1.4	3,526	6,091	+ 72.7
SMSA b	1,662	2,913	+ 75.0	3,695	6,548	+ 77.2
Buffalo	585	532	− 8.2	3,401	5,713	+ 68.0
SMSA	509	774	+ 52.1	3,494	6,455	+ 84.7
Rochester	331	318	− 4.2	3,561	6,361	+ 78.6
SMSA	155	267	+ 72.6	3,722	7,147	+ 92.0
Albany	297	278	− 6.8	3,431	5,778	+ 68.4
SMSA	291	378	+ 30.4	3,551	6,095	+ 71.6
Syracuse	221	216	− 2.1	3,471	6,247	+ 80.0
SMSA	264	347	+ 42.2	3,459	6,405	+ 85.2
Utica-Rome	101	100	− 1.1	3,268	5,873	+ 79.7
SMSA	141	178	+ 26.7	3,204	6,022	+ 88.0
Binghamton	80	76	− 5.9	3,258	6,251	+ 91.9
SMSA	104	137	+ 31.4	3,622	7,121	+ 96.6
New York State	14,830	16,782	+ 14.2	3,487	6,371	+ 82.7
All urban regions	9,508	9,213	− 3.1	3,432	5,938	+ 73.0
All nonurban regions	5,322	7,569	+ 46.1	3,484	6,581	+ 82.3

Sources: U.S. Bureau of the Census, Department of Commerce, *Statistical Abstract, 1963* (Washington, D.C.: Government Printing Office, 1964), p. 13; *U.S. Census of Population, 1950, United States Summary* (Washington, D.C.: Government Printing Office, 1952), pp. 1.156–1.160; *U.S. Census of Population, 1960, United States Summary* (Washington, D.C.: Government Printing Office, 1962), pp. 1.309–1.310; 1.338–1.341.

a All five boroughs.

b For "population," SMSA indicates only that portion of the standard metropolitan statistical area outside the central city. For "median family income," SMSA indicates the *entire* standard metropolitan statistical area.

surrounding suburban regions. Thus, it is even more revealing to observe the existing differences.

In 1950, in every region except Utica-Rome and Syracuse, median family income in the standard metropolitan statistical area is higher than it is in each respective urban center. The absolute as well as the percentage increase from 1950 through 1960 in *every* statistical area is also greater than in each corresponding urban area, and by 1960, median family income in *every* such area is higher than it is in each respective city. Similar comparisons can be made between the "all urban" and "all non-urban" regions.

Thus, with most deposits coming from local savers and with data for all deposit-receiving institutions as a group indicating a close relationship between changes in total personal income and deposit growth, the location of most mutual savings banks in large metropolitan centers (where population has been falling and where median family income has been increasingly only moderately) and the location of most savings and loan associations in nonurban regions (where population and median family income have been rising more rapidly than in the major urban areas) indicates an important reason for the different average growth rates experienced by the two industries since 1945.[18]

LOCATIONS IN OTHER MUTUAL SAVINGS BANK STATES

The situation in New York is typical of all mutual savings bank states. To demonstrate this, Table 13 records the changes in population and median family income between 1950 and 1960 in the 24 cities and 11 states that contain 91 of the 100 largest mutual savings banks.[19] In every case, population in the metropolitan area either declined or increased less rapidly than in

18 Appendix D indicates that location and local changes in population and income provide a basic explanation for the different growth rates of mutual savings banks and savings and loan associations in New York City, just as they do for all of New York State.

19 The 100 largest mutual savings banks held approximately 75 per cent of their industry's deposits throughout the post-1945 period. Thus, these institutions dominated their industry's growth rates at every regional level. Only 91 were selected for examination, because although all 100 were in large cities, only these 91 were in the largest cities of their respective states.

Assets in the savings and loan association industry are far less concentrated than in the mutual savings bank industry. Since 1945, the 100 largest savings and loan associations, for example, held less than 26 per cent of their industry's assets. Of these, only 24 were in mutual savings bank states. This was out of a total of over 3,500 savings and loan associations located throughout these states.

TABLE 13

Location of 91 of the 100 Largest Mutual Savings Banks and Percentage
Changes in Population and Median Family Income in Their
Respective Cities and States, 1950–1960

State and City of Bank Location	Number of Banks	Population, Percentage Change, 1950–60	Median Family Income, Percentage Change, 1950–60
New York		+ 14.2	82.7
Urban areas ᵃ	58	− 3.1	70.1
Massachusetts		+ 9.8	87.5
Boston	5	− 13.0	76.9
Worcester	2	− 8.3	77.2
Springfield	1	+ 7.4	73.3
Connecticut		+ 26.3	94.3
Bridgeport	3	− 1.2	78.5
Hartford	2	− 8.6	73.1
New Haven	2	− 7.5	77.6
Waterbury	1	+ 2.5	88.2
Pennsylvania		+ 7.8	97.7
Philadelphia	4	− 3.3	74.1
Pittsburgh	1	− 10.7	69.1
New Jersey		+ 25.5	84.9
Newark	2	− 7.6	65.8
Jersey City	1	− 7.7	73.7
Maryland		+ 32.3	93.2
Baltimore	3	− 1.1	72.7
New Hampshire		+ 13.8	96.0
Manchester	1	+ 6.7	n.a.
Rhode Island		+ 8.5	97.3
Providence	2	− 22.7	71.8
Delaware		+ 40.5	95.7
Wilmington	1	− 13.2	67.0
Minnesota		+ 14.5	95.7
Minneapolis	1	− 7.4	69.1
Washington		+ 19.9	78.1
Seattle	1	+ 19.1	79.4
Total	91		

Sources: U.S. Bureau of the Census, Department of Commerce, *U.S. Census of Population, 1950, United States Summary* (Washington, D.C.: Government Printing Office, 1952), pp. 1.137, 1.156–1.160, and *U.S. Census of Population, 1960, United States Summary* (Washington, D.C.: Government Printing Office, 1962), pp. 1.286, 1.309–1.310, 1.338–1.341.

ᵃ "Urban areas" for New York are defined in footnote 14, p. 82.

n.a. = Not available.

the state as a whole, and in every city (except Seattle) median family income grew less rapidly than it did throughout the state. (Disparities between the metropolitan areas and their surrounding suburban regions would, of course, be substantially greater.) Thus, 91 mutual savings banks with about 70 per cent of their industry's assets were located in regions in which increases in total personal income were comparatively small, while savings and loan associations were far more widely dispersed throughout the fastest growing regions of each state.

To compare the extent to which the two industries are concentrated in urban locations, Table 14 records both the assets and the number of institutions in each group in the most populated cities of the six states with the most mutual savings bank deposits.[20]

The table shows that in every state except Connecticut the concentration of mutual savings banks in the major metropolitan areas (i.e., the "key cities") is larger than the concentration of savings and loan associations. Excluding Connecticut, the differences between the two sets of institutions range from 12 percentage points in Massachusetts to 22 percentage points in New York. In every case, including Connecticut, the proportion of assets held by the mutual savings banks in "key cities" is higher than its counterpart for the savings and loan association industry. Differences range from 10 percentage points in Massachusetts to 89 percentage points in Pennsylvania.

Similar patterns appear when the twelve remaining mutual savings bank states are examined as a group. At the end of 1964, for example, 24 of the 89 mutual savings banks in these states held 71 per cent of the region's mutual savings bank assets. These 24 were *all* in the largest cities of their respective states—cities that since 1950 have *all* experienced population declines and advances in total personal incomes that were less rapid than those in the surrounding suburban areas. At the same time, the assets of the savings and loan associations were widely dispersed

[20] Mutual savings banks in these six states held approximately 93 per cent of their industry's assets during the post-1945 years, so the data indicate conditions that dominated the growth rates of the entire mutual savings bank industry.

TABLE 14

Number and Assets of Mutual Savings Banks and Savings and Loan Associations, Selected Cities and States, 1964 [a]

	(1)		(2)		(3)		(4)		(5)		(6)	
	Number		Number in Key Cities		(2) ÷ (1)		Assets (in billions)		Assets in Key Cities (in billions)		(4) ÷ (5)	
States	MSB	SLA	MSB	SLA	MSB	SLA	MSB	SLA	MSB	SLA	MSB	SLA
New York	125	225	78	90	62%	40%	$31,455	$7,370	$29,253	$4,495	93%	61%
Massachusetts	179	198	40	20	22	10	8,858	3,024	3,454	876	39	29
Connecticut	71	39	11	10	15	26	3,841	1,074	2,189	483	57	45
Pennsylvania	7	763	5	390	71	51	3,211	5,407	3,147	487	98	9
New Jersey	21	396	5	32	24	8	2,048	4,374	1,058	962	52	22
Maryland	6	345	5	214	83	62	744	2,039	617	347	83	17

[a] The term "key cities" refers to the urban areas listed in tables 12 and 13. In each instance, these are the largest metropolitan centers of their respective states. In every case, the growth of total personal income since 1945 in "key cities" was substantially below that of almost all other regions in each state. Figures for New York are the same as those in Table 11. All other data are from *Directory of American Savings and Loan Associations, 1965* and *Directory and Guide to the Mutual Savings Banks of the United States, 1964–65.*

among more than 3,500 organizations which were broadly spread throughout nonurban as well as urban areas.

Thus, in every region in which both types of institutions have provided savings services during the post-1945 period, the greater concentration of mutual savings bank offices and assets in the largest cities of their respective states—which in every case experienced population declines and only modest increases in average per capita income—appears to contribute an underlying explanation for the different growth rates of the two industries. Moreover, an analogous situation exists for the nation as a whole: mutual savings banks are concentrated almost entirely in the slow-growing northeastern states, while savings and loan associations are widely dispersed throughout the nation.

5

Interest Payment Differences and Growth Variance, 1945–1964

SINCE 1945, spreads between the interest payments of savings and loan associations and mutual savings banks appear to have been less important than location as a reason for the persistent differences in the average growth rates of the two groups. To support this observation, the interest payments of the two industries are compared over a wide range of geographic areas. The data indicate that, if the interest payment differentials had been the principal determinant of where people saved, mutual savings banks would surely have grown more rapidly; in some states, the growth rate spread between the two industries would have been reversed. On the other hand, the effects of interest payment competition from commercial banks and other savings media (discussed in chapter 6) have been significantly more important, especially since the mid-1950s.

The following analysis is concerned with persistent, long-term developments. In the short run, savings institutions are continually raising or lowering interest rates and are continually experiencing increases or decreases in their rates of savings growth. To many observers, these related movements suggest that changing interest payment spreads must surely be the primary determinant of different rates of savings deposits growth.[1]

---

[1] In a study of savings institutions in New York, for example, the authors conclude: "The higher rate of return offered to depositors has probably been the *most important factor* accounting for the more rapid growth of share

But over a period of months or years, many of these short-run changes offset each other as competition forces organizations to match the interest rates of their nearest rivals or, at the very least, to try to maintain fairly constant interest payment differentials.[2] Thus, by devoting attention to annual average interest payment spreads, this chapter abstracts from intra-annual changes and from the short-lived interest payment shifts of particular institutions and examines only the more persistent developments.

AVERAGE INTEREST PAYMENTS, NATIONWIDE

Table 15 indicates that from 1945 through 1964 the average interest payments made by savings and loan associations throughout the United States were consistently higher than those made by mutual savings banks, with the spread between the two sets of averages narrowing from 0.96 percentage point to 0.12 percentage point over the period. Differences widened

accounts in savings and loan associations as compared with time deposits in mutual savings banks and commercial banks" (emphasis added). Marcus Nadler and associates, *The Banking Situation in New York State* (New York: New York State Bankers Association, 1956), p. 277. This conclusion fails to explain why savings and loan associations in New York grew more rapidly than mutual savings banks from 1952 through 1956 when the average interest payments of both groups were approximately equal, and it would be even more hard pressed to explain why savings and loan association growth rates continued to exceed those of mutual savings banks from 1956 through 1964 when the average interest payments of the latter were almost constantly above those of the former. See Table 16.

2 As one study points out, with a statement equally as applicable to mutual savings banks as to savings and loan associations, after an institution raises its interest rates, "in all probability one or more of the surrounding associations would feel compelled to raise rates, thus affecting more distant associations, and the rate increase would spread. A rate reduction by one association would also be very difficult to carry out unless other associations could be persuaded to follow suit. These tendencies to avoid deposit losses and potential deposit losses are probably stronger in [an industry with] a large admixture of mutual institutions than it would be in an industry consisting only of stock corporations, as the rewards to managements of mutual organizations are far more dependent upon the size of their associations than upon their profits. In view of all these considerations, *it seems highly unlikely that associations within a given market area could differentiate their deposits on the basis of yields for any length of time.* Consequently, one would expect to find uniform rates prevailing throughout rather broadly defined geographic market areas" (emphasis added). Leo Grebler and Eugene F. Brigham, *Savings and Mortgage Markets in California* (Pasadena, Calif.: California Savings and Loan League, 1963), p. 91.

TABLE 15

Average Interest Payments of Savings and Loan Associations and
Mutual Savings Banks in the United States, 1945–1964 [a]

(*In percentages*)

Year	(1) SLA	(2) MSB	(3) (1) − (2)	Year	(1) SLA	(2) MSB	(3) (1) − (2)
1945	2.54	1.58	.96	1955	2.94	2.64	.30
1946	2.43	1.60	.83	1956	3.03	2.77	.26
1947	2.30	1.62	.68	1957	3.26	2.94	.32
1948	2.32	1.66	.66	1958	3.38	3.07	.31
1949	2.34	1.82	.52	1959	3.53	3.19	.34
1950	2.52	1.90	.62	1960	3.86	3.47	.39
1951	2.58	1.96	.62	1961	3.90	3.55	.35
1952	2.69	2.31	.38	1962	4.08	3.86	.22
1953	2.81	2.40	.41	1963	4.17	3.96	.21
1954	2.87	2.50	.37	1964	4.18	4.06	.12

Sources: United States Savings and Loan League, *Savings and Loan Fact Book, 1965*, p. 16, and National Association of Mutual Savings Banks, *National Fact Book, 1965*, p. 29.

[a] These data represent effective interest payments, i.e., payments actually distributed each year divided by the average savings on deposit during the year. Figures for savings and loan associations are for Federal Home Loan Bank System members only.

in only five of the years and remained constant during only two.

With interest payments rising almost every year, the percentage differences between the averages declined even more rapidly than the absolute differences. While the average interest payments of savings and loan associations were 61.0 per cent greater than those of mutual savings banks in 1945, the spread was less than 0.3 per cent in 1964.

Despite this substantial narrowing, savings and loan associations grew more rapidly than mutual savings banks by an average of 6.0 percentage points a year from 1946 through 1964. Contrary to what might be expected, the differences in growth rates between the two sets of institutions widened from 1945 through the mid-1950s as the interest payment differences between them narrowed; and although the difference between the growth rates declined from the mid-1950s through 1964, as would be expected, it remained greater than 4.7 percentage points until the last year of the period. In terms of the number of accounts, savings and loan associations during the 1960s grew at an average rate of 8.1 per cent annually, while the number of mutual savings bank deposits declined. For a number of reasons, however, judgment about the possible effects of differences in interest payments on the growth rates of the two types of institutions should be withheld until regions are examined where the average interest payments of mutual savings banks exceeded those of savings and loan associations for substantial periods.

NEW YORK, MASSACHUSETTS, AND CONNECTICUT

In New York, as Table 16 indicates, differences between the average interest payments of savings and loan associations and mutual savings banks fell from + .43 percentage point in 1947 to + .05 percentage point in 1954. Yet in 1954, when the average interest payments of the two types of institutions were almost equal, the growth rate differential favored the savings and loan associations by 5.4 percentage points. Then, when mutual savings bank interest payments exceeded those of savings and loan associations in eight out of the next ten years—with the two series approximately equal in 1959 and 1961—savings and loan association growth rates were greater than those of mutual savings banks every year except the last, with spreads ranging from 2.2 percentage points in 1958 to 9.8 percentage points in 1961. Moreover, from 1955 through 1964, savings and loan associations opened almost 1.2 million additional accounts (up 76 per cent), compared to a mutual savings bank gain of less than 1.0 million (up only 12 per cent). In 1962 and 1963, when the average interest payment spreads favored mutual savings banks by substantial margins, the number of savings and loan association accounts continued their persistent advance, and the number of mutual savings bank deposits *declined* by 2.4 per cent and 5.5 per cent, respectively.

In Massachusetts the situation was similar, although less dra-

TABLE 16

Average Interest Payments of Savings and Loan Associations and Mutual Savings Banks in New York, Massachusetts, and Connecticut, 1947–1964 [a]

(In percentages)

Year	New York			Massachusetts			Connecticut		
	(1) SLA	(2) MSB	(3) (1)–(2)	(4) SLA	(5) MSB	(6) (4)–(5)	(7) SLA	(8) MSB	(9) (7)–(8)
1947	1.97	1.54	.43	2.49	1.82	.67	2.17	1.90	.27
1948	2.01	1.58	.43	2.53	1.88	.65	2.22	1.88	.34
1949	2.10	1.84	.26	2.62	1.93	.69	2.31	1.90	.41
1950	2.13	1.89	.24	2.66	2.08	.58	2.28	1.99	.29
1951	2.17	1.90	.27	2.62	2.20	.42	2.38	2.12	.26
1952	2.41	2.33	.08	2.80	2.44	.36	2.41	2.31	.10
1953	2.47	2.40	.07	2.92	2.65	.27	2.63	2.36	.27
1954	2.54	2.49	.05	2.95	2.80	.15	2.58	2.42	.16
1955	2.65	2.66	−.01	2.99	2.84	.15	2.54	2.57	−.03
1956	2.77	2.81	−.04	3.02	2.86	.16	2.74	2.75	−.01
1957	2.98	3.00	−.02	3.05	2.97	.08	2.91	2.85	.06
1958	3.07	3.14	−.07	3.08	3.10	−.02	2.87	2.95	−.08
1959	3.22	3.22	.00	3.23	3.23	.00	3.19	3.43	−.24
1960	3.49	3.53	−.04	3.54	3.43	.11	3.44	3.52	−.08
1961	3.59	3.58	.01	3.66	3.66	.00	3.58	3.76	−.18
1962	3.83	3.90	−.07	3.87	3.83	.04	3.78	3.78	.00
1963	3.91	4.03	−.12	3.97	3.91	.06	3.79	3.79	.00
1964	4.04	4.16	−.12	4.00	4.00	.00	3.83	3.93	−.10

Sources: National Association of Mutual Savings Banks, *National Fact Book, 1966*, and Federal Home Loan Bank System, *Combined Financial Statements* (Washington, D.C.: Federal Home Loan Bank System, selected years).

[a] Data are interest payments actually distributed each year divided by the average savings on deposit during the year. Savings and Loan Association figures are for Federal Home Loan Bank System members only.

matic. From 1957 through 1964—when there was virtually no difference between the average interest rates of savings and loan associations and mutual savings banks—savings and loan association growth rates exceeded mutual savings bank growth rates in all but two years. In 1964—when the interest rates of the two types of institutions were equal—the growth rate differential favored the savings and loan associations by about 4 percentage points.

The comparisons for Connecticut are almost the same as those for New York: interest payment spreads favored mutual savings banks in seven of the ten years after 1954. Yet savings and loan association growth rates were greater than mutual savings bank growth rates by an average of 4 percentage points until 1964, when the growth rates were equal. Disparities with respect to the number of accounts were even greater. Thus, in these three states, which together hold over 80 per cent of all mutual savings bank deposits, whatever influence interest payment differentials between savings and loan associations and mutual savings banks may have had on their relative growth rates was apparently overshadowed by other factors.

RELATION BETWEEN INTEREST PAYMENTS
AND ADVERTISING EXPENDITURES

In many respects, interest payments and advertising expenditures are supplements. After a firm raises its interest rates, it typically increases its advertising outlays to make the public more aware of its new and higher interest levels. These outlays usually remain comparatively large as long as it seems desirable to continue attracting additional savings or until advertising costs (with respect to attracting additional funds) become higher than the expense of another interest rate increase. Because changes in interest payments and in advertising expenditures are almost always made simultaneously, it is impossible to attribute savings deposit growth clearly to one or the other. Regardless of which is assumed to be the dominant factor, however, it is clearly unrealistic to examine the effects of interest payment differentials without also considering the influence of relative advertising expenditures.[3]

Discussions on this subject typically observe that advertising outlays as a percentage of income, total assets, or deposits are invariably greater for the savings and loan association industry than for the mutual savings bank industry. Therefore, it is usually concluded that the former advertises more aggressively.[4] But with both types of institutions generally enjoying economies of size with respect to advertising costs and with advertising outlays (including "giveaways") varying widely among regions, further refinement of the data appears necessary.

Figures in Table 17—which uses 1962 as a representative post-World War II year primarily because of the availability of mutual savings bank data—indicate that in each of the three states with the largest amounts in mutual savings bank deposits the amounts spent on advertising as a percentage of gross operating income were fractionally greater for savings and loan associations than for mutual savings banks. But with the average mutual savings bank in these states ranging from two to almost eight times as large as the average savings and loan association, it is not clear that these differences are greater than those that could be expected solely on the basis of economies of size.

Furthermore, in many respects it is the amount spent on advertising, rather than the proportion of outlays to bank earnings, that influences savers. And in this respect, mutual savings banks in many regions appear to be more aggressive than savings and loan associations. In New York, for example, mutual savings banks as a group spent about three times as much on

[3] For a discussion of substitution between advertising expenditures and interest payments, see Edward S. Shaw, *Savings and Loan Structure and Market Performance* (Los Angeles: Savings and Loan Commissioner, State of California, 1962), pp. 22–25.

[4] See, for example, Gaylord A. Freeman, Jr., "Savings and Loan Competition as Seen by a Banker," *Savings and Loan Journal,* February, 1956, pp. 14–26; Lawrence L. Werboff and Marvin E. Rozen, "Market Shares and Competition among Financial Institutions," in Commission on Money and Credit, *Private Financial Institutions* (Englewood Cliffs, N.J.: Prentice-Hall, 1963), pp. 291–92; Irwin Friend, "The Effects of Monetary Policies on Nonmonetary Financial Institutions and Capital Markets," in Commission on Money and Credit, *Private Capital Markets* (Englewood Cliffs, N.J.: Prentice-Hall, 1964), pp. 31–32.

TABLE 17

Advertising Expenditures for Mutual Savings Banks and Savings and
Loan Associations in Selected States, 1962 [a]

State	Expenditures as a Percentage of Gross Operating Income		Average Size (in millions of dollars)		Total Advertising Expenditures (in thousands of dollars)		Average Advertising Expenditures (in thousands of dollars)	
	MSB	SLA	MSB	SLA	MSB	SLA	MSB	SLA
New York	1.3	1.5	173.2	23.3	11,820	4,533	93.1	19.8
Massachusetts	.9	1.5	36.9	9.1	2,801	1,708	15.5	8.4
Connecticut	1.2	1.9	41.6	18.6	1,312	832	28.5	20.8

Sources: National Association of Mutual Savings Banks, "Special Report, 1962"
(New York: National Association of Mutual Savings Banks, 1962), and Federal
Home Loan Bank Board, *Combined Financial Statements, 1962.*

[a] Figures for mutual savings banks are estimated from data for 117 out of 127
organizations in New York, 154 out of 181 in Massachusetts, and 64 out of 71 in
Connecticut.

advertising as savings and loan associations as a group. Moreover, the average mutual savings bank spent $93,100 on adver-
tising in 1962, while the average savings and loan association
spent $19,800. Thus, mutual savings banks and savings and loan
associations may be much closer than is generally realized in
terms of advertising aggressiveness, and attention is once again
directed to the importance of other factors influencing savings
deposit growth.

6

Interest Payment Competition from
Savings Alternatives

DURING THE post-1945 period, especially since the mid-1950s, interest payment competition from commercial banks and other savings media does appear to have had a significant effect on the relative growth of savings and loan associations and mutual savings banks, with mutual savings bank growth being affected to a greater extent and with differences resulting at least partially from differences in location.

COMMERCIAL BANK INTEREST PAYMENTS

The intense competition for savings during the post-World War II period did not begin until the mid-1950s. In the years immediately following the war, commercial banks met their traditional credit demands and expanded consumer loans as well by relying primarily on the growth of demand deposits and on their ability to convert U.S. Government bonds into loanable funds on an as-needed basis.[1] These institutions made virtually no effort to attract savings during this period, and the average

---

[1] From 1945 through 1951, for example, loans extended by all commercial banks rose by more than $31.7 billion. At the same time, demand deposits increased $23.3 billion, holdings of U.S. Government bonds were reduced by $29.1 billion—the loan-to-deposit ratio advanced from 17 per cent to 35 per cent—and time and savings deposits climbed by $7.8 billion. Board of Governors of the Federal Reserve System, *Supplement to Banking and Monetary Statistics*, October, 1962), p. 23.

interest payments on their time and savings accounts remained
below 1 per cent until 1951 even though the legal ceiling was
2½ per cent. At the same time, yields on U.S. Government
bonds, used in this chapter as an indication of what was happening to long-term interest rates on all types of securities, were
kept artificially low by an agreement between the Treasury and
the Federal Reserve.

By the early 1950s, however, it was becoming increasingly
clear that commercial banks were going to have to rely more
and more heavily on time and savings deposits for loanable
funds as well as for growth. The desirability of limiting the
increases of demand deposits as an anti-inflationary measure,
combined with the 1951 "accord" ending the Federal Reserve's
obligation to support U.S. Government bond prices, indicated
that "forces tending to curtail sharply the ability of the banking
system to keep pace with the growth of the economy as a whole,
via increasing demand deposits, were already developing in the
early postwar period." [2] It was becoming clear, moreover, that
liquid assets were far from being an inexhaustible source of
loanable funds and that " 'loaned up' was not a theoretical concept, but a point which the banking system could, in fact, reach,
and, more importantly, toward which it was heading." [3]

Thus, the commercial banking system as well as the major
capital markets entered the fifties with the seeds of competition
already sown—competition that was to have different effects on
the growth of the mutual savings bank and savings and loan
association industries as a result of locational differences between the two types of institutions.

Economic problems accompanying the Korean conflict and
the subsequent recession kept the Federal Reserve from pur-
suing a tight money policy. It was not until mid-1955 that the
growth of demand deposits dropped off somewhat and that interest rates began rising rapidly. Then commercial banks found
their traditional source of funds drying up just as the demand

[2] American Bankers Association, Savings Division, *Response to Change: A Century of Commercial Bank Activity in the Savings Field* (New York: American
Bankers Association, 1965), p. 66.
[3] *Ibid.*

for funds was increasing. Thus it became apparent that if these institutions were to maintain their relative position in an expanding economy they would have to turn increasingly to the savings market.

Concurrently, other types of financial organizations were faced with the same expanding demand for loanable funds and were also stepping up their efforts to attract savings. Interest rates on time and savings deposits in commercial banks had to be pushed steadily higher to meet the competition. By the end of 1956 some of the larger commercial banks were pressing on the 2½ per cent ceiling established by Regulation Q of the Federal Reserve. Still the need and competition for savings continued. Finally, on January 1, 1957 these pressures resulted in Regulation Q being raised for the first time in over twenty years.

TABLE 18

Maximum Rates Payable on Time and Savings Deposits under Federal Reserve Regulation Q

(Per cent per annum)

	Effective Date					
Type and Maturity of Deposit	*Jan. 1, 1936*	*Jan. 1, 1957*	*Jan. 1, 1962*	*July 17, 1963*	*Nov. 24, 1964*	*Dec. 6, 1965*
Savings deposits:						
1 year or more	2½	3	4	4	4	4
Less than 1 year	2½	3	3½	3½	4	4
Other time deposits:						
1 year or more	2½	3	4	4	4½	5½
6 months–1 year	2½	3	3½	4	4½	5½
90 days–6 months	2	2½	2½	4	4½	5½
Less than 90 days (30–89 days)	1	1	1	1	4	5½

Source: Board of Governors of the Federal Reserve System, *Federal Reserve Bulletin*, April, 1966, p. 545.

The commercial banking system was quick to take advantage of the higher interest rate ceilings. Average interest payments rose 0.5 percentage point in 1957—as much as the entire advance of the previous five years (see Table 19). At the same time, the annual net growth rate of time and savings deposits more than doubled, exceeding 8 per cent for the first time in post-1945 history. Moreover, as discussed below, interest payment spreads between commercial banks on the one hand and savings and loan associations and mutual savings banks on the other hand were also reduced, as were the growth rates of the latter two types of intermediaries. Thus, 1957 marks a turning point in commercial bank competition for savings in terms of interest payment increases, higher growth rates, and effect on the growth of competing institutions.

TABLE 19

Average Interest Payments on Time and Savings Deposits and
Net Growth Rates of Commercial Banks, 1947–1964 [a]

(In percentages)

Year	Average Interest Payments	Net Growth Rates	Year	Average Interest Payments	Net Growth Rates
1947	0.9	3.0	1956	1.6	3.2
1948	0.9	0.1	1957	2.1	8.5
1949	0.9	− 0.5	1958	2.2	9.3
1950	0.9	− 0.5	1959	2.4	2.3
1951	1.1	2.8	1960	2.6	4.0
1952	1.1	6.2	1961	2.8	8.3
1953	1.1	5.6	1962	3.1	15.2
1954	1.3	5.0	1963	3.3	9.1
1955	1.4	2.2	1964	3.5	8.8

[a] Effective interest payments are based on data from the Federal Deposit Insurance Corporation, *Annual Report,* 1947–64. Net growth rates exclude interest payments.

From 1957 through 1961, forces continued to dampen the growth of demand deposits, thereby providing commercial banks with an incentive to continue competing aggressively for time and savings deposits.[4] As Table 19 indicates, average interest payments on these accounts were persistently increased.

[4] Demand deposits increased by only 2.3 per cent from 1957 through 1961; time and savings deposits rose by 9.0 per cent. For a detailed year-by-year account of commercial bank competition for savings during this period, see *ibid.*, pp. 75–82; see also Norman Strunk, "Commercial Banks Come Alive," *Savings and Loan News,* September, 1965, pp. 18–26.

By 1961, many commercial banks found themselves once again pressing on the legal maximum.[5]

Regulation Q was liberalized again in 1962, and many commercial banks responded by immediately increasing their interest payments. During that year, the industry's average interest rate climbed to 3.1 per cent, and perhaps even more important, many of these organizations, particularly the larger ones, began to advertise a full 4 per cent for the first time in the postwar period. The net growth of time and savings deposits soared to over 15 per cent that year, and the $14.2 billion savings gain is the largest increase in commercial banking history. At the same time, interest payment spreads between commercial banks on the one hand and savings and loan associations and mutual savings banks on the other hand fell to the lowest levels in more than a quarter of a century.

Other increases in Regulation Q in 1963, 1964, and 1965 brought similar changes, and it remains to relate these developments to the growth rates of the savings and loan association and mutual savings bank industries.

COMMERCIAL BANK COMPETITION, NATIONWIDE

Some of the differential effects of the increased competition from commercial banks in the years following the "accord" between the Treasury and the Federal Reserve System are suggested by data in Chart 7. Annual growth rates of savings and loan associations and mutual savings banks are on the ordinate, and spreads between the average interest payments of the two industries on the one hand and commercial banks on the other hand are on the abscissa. Figures are for 1952 through 1964.[6]

[5] Upon reaching the interest payment ceiling, many commercial banks began computing interest on a daily basis. New innovations were developed to attract still more savings deposits. Perhaps the most successful were the secondary market that made time certificates of deposit effectively, as well as theoretically, negotiable and reduction in the size of the certificates to amounts attractive to individual savers.

[6] The commercial bank interest payments used to compute the spreads with respect to savings and loan associations are the average interest payments made on time and savings deposits at the end of each year by members of the Federal Reserve System. The figures for savings and loan associations are those in Table 15. Commercial bank interest payments used to compute the spreads with respect

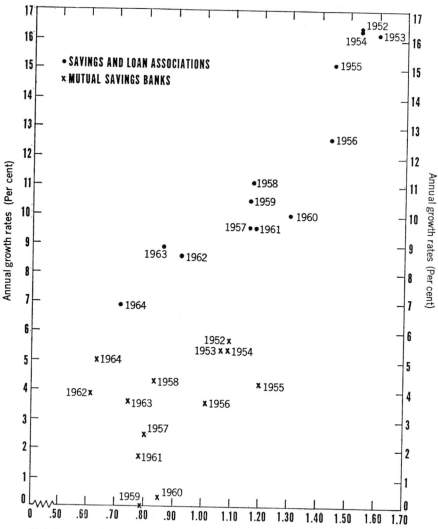

CHART 7

Net Growth Rates of Savings and Loan Associations and
Mutual Savings Banks and Interest Payment
Spreads over Commercial Banks in the
United States, 1952–1964

SLA interest rates – CB interest rates; MSB interest rates – CB interest rates
(percentage points).

Sources: Table 15, Appendix B; Federal Deposit Insurance Corporation,
Annual Report, selected issues.

At least five observations can be made about the savings and loan association data:

1) For 1952 through 1956, savings and loan association growth rates all exceeded 12 per cent, with an average slightly greater than 15 per cent.

2) In 1957, with the first increase in Regulation Q in over twenty years, many commercial banks raised their interest payments, and the interest payment spread between savings and loan associations and commercial banks declined by more than a quarter of a percentage point. Concurrently, the savings and loan association industry's growth rate fell sharply, while that of the commercial bank industry rose to what was then its highest level since World War II. In many cases, interest payment differentials between individual savings and loan associations and their nearest commercial bank competitors fell below 1 percentage point—into the range in which interest payment competition from commercial banks is traditionally thought to begin affecting the decisions of a substantial margin of savers.[7]

to mutual savings banks are weighted averages composed of year-end figures for time and savings deposits held by Federal Reserve members in the New York Reserve City (weighted at 49 per cent), that portion of the New York Reserve District outside New York City (9 per cent), the Boston and Philadelphia Reserve Districts (38 per cent), and the San Francisco and Richmond Reserve Districts (4 per cent). The weighting of these regions approximates the distribution of mutual savings bank deposits and therefore yields an average of commercial bank interest payments weighted in accordance with the degree to which there is close competition with mutual savings banks. The figures for mutual savings banks are those in Table 15.

Even with this weighting system, the observations in Chart 7 and in all subsequent charts in this section understate the impact of commercial bank competition on the growth of mutual savings banks and overstate the effect on the growth of savings and loan associations. In all regions, most mutual savings bank offices are located in the major metropolitan centers, where they compete most directly with the largest commercial banks, organizations which typically pay the highest interest rates in their industry. Savings and loan associations, on the other hand, are dispersed more widely throughout each region and therefore compete less directly with the largest and most aggressive commercial banks.

7 It is often observed: "[A] rule of thumb commonly held in the savings and loan business is that associations need a 0.5 per cent to 1 per cent rate advantage over commercial banks to compensate savers for surmounting a psychological hurdle regarding the relative safety and convenience of the two types of institutions." Leon T. Kendall, *The Savings and Loan Business* (Englewood Cliffs, N.J.: Prentice-Hall, 1962), p. 33. More important than the "psychological hurdle," of course, is the need to compensate savers for giving up the advantages of the "one-stop" or "full-service" facilities offered by commercial banks.

3) From 1957 through 1961, interest payment spreads between the two types of institutions remained below 1.3 percentage points, and although personal savings and the amounts held in deposit-receiving institutions both increased substantially, savings and loan association growth rates remained well below levels of the previous five years.

4) A similar situation occurred in 1962. Regulation Q was again liberalized; the average interest payment spread between savings and loan associations and commercial banks fell sharply; the commercial bank growth rate soared to a new post-1945 high; and the savings and loan association growth rate dropped to a new low.

5) The pattern was repeated again in 1964.

Thus, interest payment competition between savings and loan associations and commercial banks appears to have had a substantial influence on the growth of the former, especially since the mid-1950s, and it is not without reason that one of the leading spokesmen for the savings and loan association industry recently observed: "The most important new fact of life in the savings and loan business has been the emergence of commercial banking as a strong, competitive force." [8]

Turning to mutual savings bank growth rates and interest payment spreads over commercial banks, at least three observations can be made from the data in Chart 7:

1) The average interest payment spreads between mutual savings banks and commercial banks are predominantly on the left-hand side of the diagram: in only one instance is the interest payment spread between the two types of institutions larger than 1.15 percentage point. Meanwhile, interest payment spreads between savings and loan associations and commercial banks are under 1.15 percentage point in only three of the thirteen observations—the three in which savings and loan association growth rates are lowest. This is at least partially because most mutual savings banks are located in large urban and financial centers

[8] Norman Strunk, "Commercial Banks Come Alive," *Savings and Loan News*, September, 1965, pp. 18–26.

where they compete directly with the largest and most aggressive commercial banks—and the commercial bank interest rates are weighted to reflect this fact (see footnote 6)—while savings and loan associations are more widely dispersed.

2) Even in the relatively narrow range within which interest payment differentials between mutual savings banks and commercial banks fluctuate, there is some evidence of movements similar to those experienced by savings and loan associations: from 1952 through 1956; mutual savings bank growth rates averaged 5 per cent; then, in 1957, the spread between the average mutual savings bank and commercial bank interest payments dropped by about one third of a percentage point and the mutual savings bank growth rate also fell, although only by about 1 percentage point. From that year to the present, however, no simple relationship between mutual savings bank growth and competition from commercial banks is apparent from the data in Chart 7, except perhaps that both the growth rates and the interest payment differentials remained relatively low.

3) Even when interest payment spreads over commercial banks are the same or approximately the same for both savings and loan associations and mutual savings banks, the growth rates of the former are invariably greater.[9] This redirects attention to the importance of different locations and to factors

9 Even when the interest payment spreads over commercial banks are the same for savings and loan associations and mutual savings banks, the percentage differences favor the latter. This is because interest payments for all types of institutions rose throughout the post-1945 period, while in every case the interest payment spreads between savings and loan associations and commercial banks narrowed later than the interest payment spreads between mutual savings banks and commercial banks. Thus, for example, the interest payment spread between mutual savings banks and commercial banks was about 1.2 percentage point in 1955, a difference of 90 per cent. The interest payment spread between savings and loan associations and commercial banks did not narrow to 1.2 percentage point until 1961 however, and by that time—owing to constantly rising levels of interest payments—the spread was only 42 per cent. Despite the fact that the interest payment spreads between mutual savings banks and commercial banks were larger in percentage terms than those between savings and loan associations and commercial banks—even when absolute differences were the same for the two types of intermediaries—the growth rates of savings and loan associations were always above those of mutual savings banks.

conducive to savings deposit growth within the areas being served.

Thus, the declining spread between savings and loan association and mutual savings bank growth rates since the mid-1950s is not the result of a resurgence of mutual savings bank growth but rather of slower savings and loan association growth that seems at least partially related to increased competition from commercial banks.

COMPETITION WITH BOND YIELDS

The net flow of savings into mutual savings banks and savings and loan associations is sensitive to changes in over-all business conditions and to movements in capital markets as well as to fluctuations in the relative attractiveness of competing savings institutions. But while it seems reasonable to assume that mutual savings banks and savings and loan associations are affected similarly by broad changes in the patterns of consumption, savings, and over-all business activity, locational differences suggest that it is also reasonable to expect mutual savings banks to be more sensitive than savings and loan associations to movements in capital markets. The National Association of Mutual Savings Banks points out a reason for this:

A large proportion of total savings bank deposits is located in the major financial centers—more than 55 per cent in New York, Philadelphia, and Boston—where the impact of Federal Reserve monetary policies and capital market changes is felt most rapidly and powerfully. By contrast, savings and loan associations operate in all 50 states, and a substantial segment of the industry is located in smaller urban areas, less sensitive to money market changes than the major financial centers.[10]

The following pages test this statement by examining data for selected regions. At the outset, however, it can be noted that if the above observation is correct—considering that bond yields are typically more attractive during periods of prosperity and

[10] National Association of Mutual Savings Banks, *Annual Report: Facts and Figures, 1964*, p. 30.

that there were fifteen and a half years of prosperity and only three and a half of recession from October, 1945, through October, 1964—confinement to their present locations imposes an obvious disadvantage on mutual savings banks. Moreover, increases in the size of the average deposit and in the proportion of large, interest-sensitive accounts held by mutual savings banks indicate that shifting funds between these institutions and capital market instruments can be expected to become increasingly common in the future.

Nationwide

Chart 8 compares the net savings flows into mutual savings banks and savings and loan associations with spreads between the average interest rates of the two industries and the average yields on three- to five-year U.S. Government bonds. Seasonally adjusted quarterly data are recorded for 1949 through 1962, and yields on Government bonds are used as an indication of what was happening to long-term rates on all types of securities. Dollars are on the left-hand ordinate to measure savings flows, while basis points (100 basis points equal 1 percentage point) are on the right-hand ordinate to measure interest payment spreads. The business cycle reference dates are those set by the National Bureau of Economic Research.

The chart shows that net savings flows into savings and loan associations increased during every recession as differences widened between their average interest payments and bond yields. But with only a few short-lived exceptions, net savings flows into savings and loan associations also rose during years of expansion, when differences generally *narrowed* between their interest payments and bond yields. Savings flows into mutual savings banks also advanced during each recession as differences widened between their interest payments and bond yields. However, savings inflows declined almost every year that spreads over bond yields narrowed. The only major exceptions were 1951 and 1952, when mutual savings bank deposits increased as the buying spree during the early part of the Korean

Chart 8
Net Savings Flows into Mutual Savings Banks and Savings
and Loan Associations and Interest Payment Spreads
over Average Yields on Three- to Five-Year U.S.
Government Bonds, 1949–1962

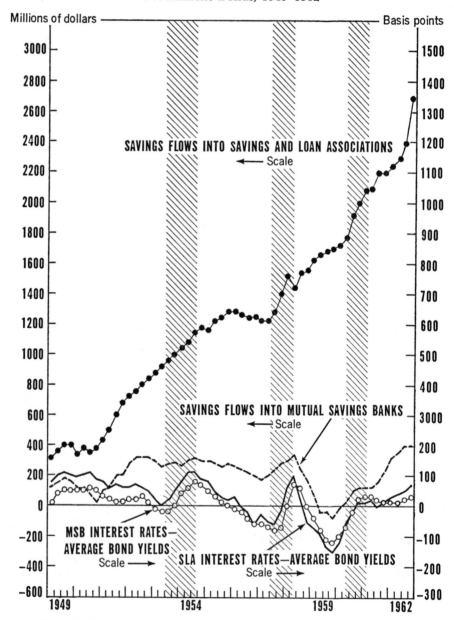

Note: Savings data are net interest payments, seasonally adjusted, quarterly figures. Shaded areas represent recession periods, according to National Bureau of
Economic Research chronology.

Sources: National Association of Mutual Savings Banks; United States Savings
and Loan League; Board of Governors of the Federal Reserve System, *Federal
Reserve Bulletin,* selected issues.

War subsided. There was also a short-lived exception during the second half of 1961 as some of the larger New York City mutual savings banks improved their interest payment spreads over commercial banks. The generally direct relationship between changes in yield spreads and savings flows can be observed in Chart 8. Thus, industrywide data appear consistent with the National Association of Mutual Savings Banks' observation that savings flows into mutual savings banks are more sensitive to changes in bond yields than are savings flows into savings and loan associations. This can be seen more clearly, however, in the data for smaller geographic regions.

New York

Data for New York State, New York City, and that portion of New York State outside of New York City are generally consistent with the conclusions of the previous section.

Chart 9 relates net savings flows from 1950 through 1962 for mutual savings banks and savings and loan associations in New York State to spreads between their average interest payments and average bond yields. The easily observable patterns are similar in many respects to those for industrywide data: net savings flows into mutual savings banks appear closely related to changes in the spread between their interest rates and bond yields, while net savings flows into savings and loan associations seem independent of changes in the difference between their interest payments and bond yields. With approximately 80 per cent of all New York State's mutual savings bank deposits in New York City, compared to only 50 per cent for savings and loan associations, this is exactly what would be expected on the basis of the hypothesis that the closer an organization is to a major financial center the greater its sensitivity to movements in the capital markets.

Charts 10 and 11 reveal this relationship even more clearly. Chart 10 records data for New York City from 1957 through 1962. Mutual savings banks, being more heavily concentrated in Manhattan than savings and loan associations, display greater sensitivity to changing bond yields. This is particularly clear in

CHART 9

Net Savings Flows into Mutual Savings Banks and Savings
and Loan Associations in New York and Interest
Payment Spreads over Average Yields on Three-
to Five-Year U.S. Government Bonds,
1950–1962

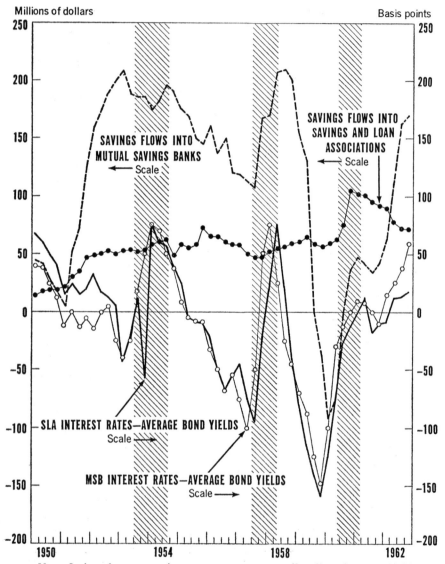

Note: Savings data are net interest payments, seasonally adjusted, quarterly figures. Shaded areas represent recession periods, according to National Bureau of
Economic Research chronology.

Sources: Savings Banks Association of New York State; Savings Association
League of New York State; Board of Governors of the Federal Reserve System,
Federal Reserve Bulletin, selected issues.

1959 when the declining yield differential is accompanied by a net decline in mutual savings bank deposits while quarterly savings flows into savings and loan associations remain essentially unchanged.

Chart 11 relates the same variables for organizations located in the portion of New York State outside New York City. If proximity to bond markets is a basic determinant of sensitivity to changes in bond yields, net savings flows to institutions outside New York City should be less responsive than net savings flows to organizations within New York City. Moreover, considering that mutual savings banks are more highly concentrated in the state's largest cities (even excluding New York City), it would be expected that they would display more sensitivity than savings and loan associations to changing bond yields.

Data in Chart 11 indicate that both of these conditions are met: savings flows into mutual savings banks outside New York City are observably less sensitive to competition from bond yields than are savings flows into New York City organizations (compare Chart 10 and Chart 11). Furthermore, savings flows into mutual savings banks outside New York City are somewhat more closely related than savings flows into savings and loan associations to changing interest rate differentials. This is particularly clear in the 1959 decline.

Thus, data for New York State, New York City, and the region outside New York City, as well as nationwide figures, all support the thesis that sensitivity to bond yields is stronger in the major financial centers than in outlying areas. Attention is directed to still another disadvantage that mutual savings banks have faced during the post-1945 period by being located predominantly in large financial centers while savings and loan associations have been more widely dispersed throughout the nation and outside financial centers.

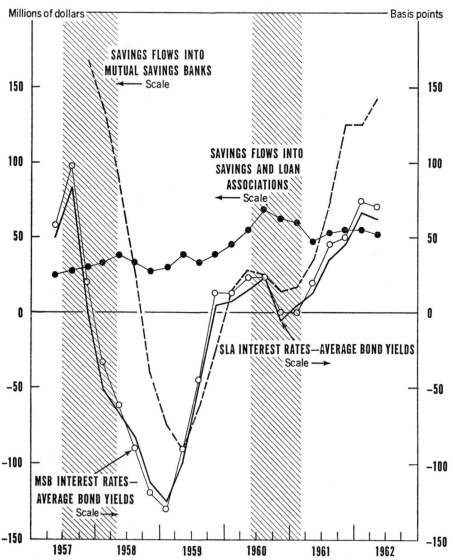

CHART 10
Net Savings Flows into Mutual Savings Banks and Savings
and Loan Associations in New York City and Interest
Payment Spreads over Average Yields on Three-
to Five-Year U.S. Government Bonds,
1957-II to 1962-II

Note: Savings data are net interest payments, seasonally adjusted, quarterly figures. Shaded areas represent recession periods, according to National Bureau of
Economic Research chronology.

Sources: Savings Banks Association of New York State; Savings Association
League of New York State; Board of Governors of the Federal Reserve System,
Federal Reserve Bulletin, selected issues.

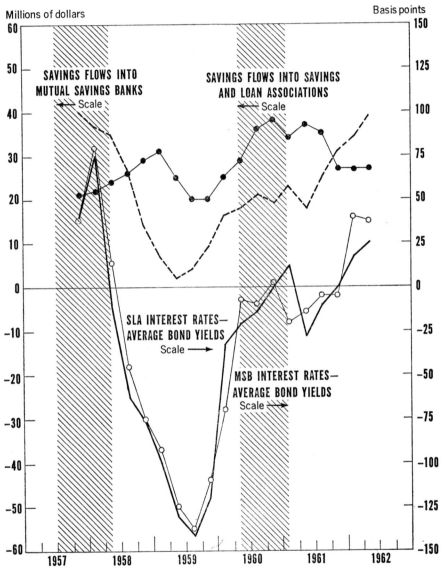

CHART 11
Net Savings Flows into Mutual Savings Banks and Savings
and Loan Associations in New York State Excluding
New York City and Interest Payment Spreads
over Average Yields on Three- to Five-
Year U.S. Government Bonds,
1957-IV to 1962-II

Millions of dollars   Basis points

SAVINGS FLOWS INTO
MUTUAL SAVINGS BANKS
→ Scale

SAVINGS FLOWS INTO SAVINGS
AND LOAN ASSOCIATIONS
← Scale

SLA INTEREST RATES—
AVERAGE BOND YIELDS
Scale →

MSB INTEREST RATES—
AVERAGE BOND YIELDS
Scale →

Note: Savings data are net interest payments, seasonally adjusted, quarterly figures. Shaded areas represent recession periods, according to National Bureau of
Economic Research chronology.

Sources: Savings Banks Association of New York State; Savings Association
League of New York State; Board of Governors of the Federal Reserve System,
Federal Reserve Bulletin, selected issues.

7

Safety and Liquidity as Factors in Growth

ALTHOUGH ATTITUDES toward safety and liquidity vary from saver to saver and over time as well, this chapter indicates that, in terms of both factors, mutual savings bank deposits during the post-1945 period have generally been considered preferable or equal to—but never less desirable than—savings and loan association accounts. As confidence in savings and loan associations started to return after their heavy losses and liquidity problems of the 1930s, shifting preferences undoubtedly advanced their growth rates above what they would otherwise have been. When savings and loan associations are compared with mutual savings banks, however, it becomes clear that differences in attitudes toward safety or liquidity do not provide an explanation for the consistently higher growth rates of the former since 1945.

SAFETY DURING THE 1930s

Mutual savings banks have a safety record unrivaled by any other deposit-receiving industry. There were no mutual savings bank failures during the 1930s, and although the value of their investments declined substantially, they passed almost no losses on to the depositors.

To a great extent, these developments were made possible by

the comparatively conservative investment policies that mutual savings banks followed during the 1920s. By having sufficient cash and secondary liquidity to honor almost all their withdrawal requests upon demand in the early 1930s—while thousands of savings and loan associations and commercial banks were failing—these institutions generated such confidence among savers that the result was a net savings inflow almost every year of the depression decade.[1] This inflow, in turn, allowed mutual savings banks to continue honoring their withdrawal demands, while eliminating most of the need for an immediate liquidation of assets.

The savings and loan association record was very different. As Table 20 indicates, 1,706 associations failed during the 1930s, and losses passed directly on to savers have been estimated at $200,400,000. In addition, substantial losses were realized by hundreds of thousands—possibly millions—of persons who, in

TABLE 20

Savings and Loan Association Failures and Estimated
Losses to Shareholders, 1930–1939

Year	Number of SLA Failures	Total Liability of Failed SLA (in thousands of dollars)	Estimated Losses to Shareholders (in thousands of dollars)
1930	190	80,430	24,676
1931	126	61,909	22,328
1932	122	52,818	20,337
1933	88	215,517	43,955
1934	68	34,728	10,174
1935	239	31,946	15,782
1936	144	20,316	9,052
1937	269	44,739	15,775
1938	277	36,025	11,281
1939	183	84,901	27,040
Total	1,706	663,329	200,400

Source: Leon T. Kendall, *The Savings and Loan Business* (Englewood Cliffs, N.J.: Prentice-Hall, 1962), p. 142.

[1] See Chart 3.

their need for immediate cash, sold their savings accounts at a discount. In many cities,

A well-organized market for the shares of building and loan associations developed, and quote sheets similar to those appearing for common stocks on the financial pages of today's newspapers were published by brokerage firms . . . [showing] rather clearly that shares usually were sold at discounts of 20 per cent to 30 per cent.[2]

Thus, to the extent that public confidence diminishes as losses increase, saver confidence clearly favored mutual savings banks and worked against the growth of savings and loan associations during the early 1930s.

LIQUIDITY DURING THE 1930s

Even though they were legally entitled to require a 30- to 90-day written notice, mutual savings banks honored almost all withdrawal requests upon demand throughout the 1930s. The major exceptions occurred when these institutions were closed for the national banking holiday in March, 1933, during similar holidays declared by particular states, and in Pennsylvania—where for a number of years it was mandatory to require a 30-day notice before permitting withdrawals. A few organizations in other states also required notice periods from time to time, but these instances were few and short-lived.[3]

The situation was significantly different for savings and loan associations. By the 1930s, almost all of these institutions were honoring withdrawal requests upon demand; in fact, it was widely assumed that this was an integral part of the savings service. Unlike mutual savings banks, however, most savings and loan associations relied heavily on borrowing and on the possibility of borrowing from commercial banks to meet their liquidity needs. As one writer observes:

[2] Leon T. Kendall, *The Savings and Loan Business* (Englewood Cliffs, N.J.: Prentice-Hall, 1962), p. 143.

[3] As with attitudes toward safety, the fact that almost all mutual savings banks were meeting their withdrawal demands upon request contributed to confidence among savers and thus to the net savings inflow received by most of these institutions almost every year of the depression. This, of course, helped forestall potential liquidity crises.

As a matter of tradition and in order to maintain high cash earnings, associations sought and boasted of a low cash position. This low cash position was partly made possible by extensive use of short-term borrowing from commercial banks. It is estimated that in the 1930s, just before the general credit deflation, the associations had nearly $400,000,000 borrowed on short term from commercial banks. At the same time, it was customary for associations to meet all requests for withdrawals on demand.[4]

Thus, as Table 21 indicates, very few savings and loan associations held large liquid reserves in 1930. While the average liquidity ratio for mutual savings banks was 8.7 per cent during that year, the ratio for savings and loan associations was only 3.2 per cent.

TABLE 21

Liquidity Ratios of the Mutual Savings Bank and Savings and
Loan Association Industries, Selected Years [a]

(In percentages)

Year End	Mutual Savings Banks	Savings and Loan Associations
1930	8.7	3.2
1940	34.8	8.6
1945	66.2	36.9
1950	58.2	17.2
1955	33.4	13.7
1960	19.6	11.7
1964	13.9	10.8

Sources: United States Savings and Loan League, *Savings and Loan Fact Book* and National Association of Mutual Savings Banks, *Annual Report: Facts and Figures,* selected issues.

[a] Liquidity ratios are cash plus U.S. government securities divided by total savings.

As long as savings and loan associations were receiving a net savings inflow and as long as commercial banks were extending the necessary loans, most withdrawal requests were honored upon demand. But in late 1929 and during the early 1930s—

[4] Morton Bodfish, "Depression Experience of Savings and Loan Associations in the United States," Address delivered in Salzburg, Austria, before the Fifth International Congress of Savings, Building, and Loan Associations, September, 1935, p. 7.

precisely when withdrawal requests were rising rapidly and savings inflows were declining sharply—commercial banks, beset with liquidity problems of their own, began refusing to extend short-term loans to savings and loan associations. Moreover, many stopped refinancing existing loans. To make matters still worse, it was not unusual to find that:

The moment any city or town experienced a [commercial] bank closing, the savings and loan associations were immediately besieged with withdrawal demands and forced on notice. When an association went on notice, new savings or investments usually stopped entirely. As soon as the [commercial] bank began to be distressed, it called for payment of its advances to associations. . . . Thus did the demands for cash pile up and the receipts of cash diminish in nearly every association located within range of a commercial bank failure.[5]

Consequently:

In virtually every area in which a savings and loan association failed or was closed, one or more commercial banks in that area had closed previously. By the same token, it is generally true that in areas where commercial banks remained open, most, if not all, of the savings and loan associations also remained open.[6]

Of course, in many cases the liquidity problems faced by savings and loan associations were compounded as much if not more by their previous investment practices as by their inability to borrow short-term funds from commercial banks.

Because it had been customary for savings and loan associations to honor all withdrawal demands upon request, confidence in the liquidity of these institutions dropped sharply when they no longer did so. In many cases, savings inflows decreased substantially or stopped, and often it was just a matter of time before the institution failed.

SAFETY SINCE THE FORMATION OF THE FDIC AND FSLIC

By the time the Federal Deposit Insurance Corporation (FDIC) was formed, in 1933, mutual savings banks had already demonstrated their ability to provide adequate safety for their deposits. Their excellent record has continued down to the

5 *Ibid.,* p. 11.
6 Kendall, *The Savings and Loan Business,* p. 141.

present, and there is every reason to assume that saver confidence in the safety of mutual savings bank deposits has remained consistently high regardless of whether past performance, present conditions, or expectations are considered.[7]

After the FDIC had been organized, many savings and loan association officials felt that their organizations had been placed at a disadvantage with respect to the public's image of the comparative safety of different types of deposit-receiving institutions. Thus, they designed a similar type of insurance agency for their industry, and it was largely along these lines that Congress formed the Federal Savings and Loan Insurance Corporation (FSLIC) in 1934.[8] Since then the FSLIC has rendered assistance to over fifty institutions, and as a result of this assistance as well as some direct payments to savers, no affiliated savings and loan association has ever had to pass on a loss to any of its savers. With respect to actual performance, therefore, insured savings and loan associations and mutual savings banks have always offered complete (and therefore equal) safety to savers.[9]

[7] When the FDIC was organized, all mutual savings banks automatically were made members for a 90-day trial period. When the three months ended, however, almost all these banks immediately withdrew. It was widely asserted that they did not care to participate in an organization that appeared to be dominated by commercial banking interests and through which government officials were given the authority to impose "unnecessary" restraints on the mutual savings banking industry. Subsequently, mutual savings bankers formed their own insurance agencies in New York, Massachusetts, and Connecticut. The New York plan was terminated in 1943 and the Connecticut plan in 1960. Today all mutual savings banks are affiliated with either the FDIC or the Mutual Savings Bank Central Fund of Massachusetts.

For history of the early years of the FDIC and the development of the various state insurance plans, see Adolf A. Berle, *The Bank That Banks Built* (New York: Harper & Brothers, 1959), pp. 1–34, 63–74.

[8] When plans for organizing the FSLIC were first presented, strong opposition developed from the mutual savings bank and commercial bank industries. At the same time, savings and loan association officials were strongly opposed to the proposed FHA program to insure certain types of residential mortgages. They felt that this program would induce mutual savings banks and commercial banks to increase their participation in the mortgage market under the umbrella of federal insurance. As a compromise, savings and loan association officials received the FSLIC as part of the Home Owner's Loan Act that simultaneously created the FHA. For additional information, see Josephine Ewalt, *A Business Reborn* (Chicago: United States Savings and Loan League, 1961), chapter VI.

[9] From the standpoint of a saver, the degree to which a savings deposit is considered safe depends on the extent to which it is felt that the return of the full amount is assured. Complete safety, in this context, means it is felt that the entire amount will surely be returned in cash.

But as Table 22 indicates, not all savings and loan associations joined the FSLIC immediately. Some could not meet membership requirements; others did not care to join. By 1940, however, over half the industry's assets were held by insured institutions, and by the end of World War II this figure had risen to 70 per cent.

TABLE 22

Number and Assets of Savings and Loan Associations Affiliated with the Federal Savings and Loan Insurance Corporation, Selected Years

Year End	Number of Insured Institutions	Total Assets (in millions of dollars)	Assets of Insured SLA to Industry Total (in percentages)
1935	1,117	711	12.1
1940	2,277	2,926	51.0
1945	2,475	6,123	·70.0
1950	2,860	13,664	81.0
1955	3,554	34,074	90.6
1960	4,098	67,430	94.2
1964	4,463	114,652	96.2

Source: United States Savings and Loan League, *Savings and Loan Fact Book, 1965*, p. 123.

The rapid growth of the savings and loan association industry, especially those institutions affiliated with the FSLIC, indicates that public confidence in the safety of savings accounts was rapidly restored. Despite the failure of over 1,700 savings and loan associations during the 1930s and the loss of millions of dollars by shareholders, savings accounts rose by $2.7 billion (57 per cent) from 1941 through 1945, while mutual savings bank deposits increased by $4.8 billion (only 46 per cent). The number of accounts in savings and loan associations advanced by 1.2 million (19 per cent) during the four years, while the number in mutual savings banks increased by only 1.1 million (7 per cent).[10]

[10] It has been suggested that during and after World War II there may have been a shift in the degree of risk savers were willing to assume (owing to factors such as the higher levels of income, the growth of personal savings, and the

Moreover, as the savings and loan association industry grew by $2.7 billion, the assets of organizations affiliated with the FSLIC increased by exactly the same amount. Some of this growth, of course, resulted from the addition of institutions to the FSLIC, but for the most part it indicates that almost all savings were going into insured organizations. Thus, the FSLIC clearly played a major part in the restoration of saver confidence in the safety of savings and loan associations. But in the minds of many savers memories of depression experiences remained vivid and still further shifts of confidence were to take place during the post-World War II period.

Safety Provisions, 1945–1964

Savings and loan associations, like almost all other types of financial institutions, emerged from World War II with highly liquid investment portfolios. Approximately 33 per cent of total assets were in cash and U.S. Government bonds. The remainder was primarily in amortized, first mortgages on one- to four-family homes.[11] After 1945, to recapitulate briefly, the proportion of the industry's investments in residential mortgages began to increase almost immediately; by 1950, more than 77 per cent of all assets were in home financing loans, and this figure has fluctuated between 77 and 80 per cent down to the present. Thus, one way to evaluate the safety of savings accounts since 1945 is to examine the safety of these investments, including an analysis of

---

increase in the liquid assets of individuals) and that this might explain the relatively rapid growth of savings and loan associations during recent years. See David and Charlotte Alhadeff, "The Struggle for Commercial Bank Savings," *Quarterly Journal of Economics*, LXXII (February, 1958), 1–22.

But it has also been observed: "The difficulty with [the Alhadeffs'] argument can perhaps be expressed in the question: Is it the amount of risk people are willing to assume or the amount of risk they think they are assuming which has changed? Surely it is a strange point to find in a discussion of thrift that people are willing to shoulder greater risk, because for this type of financial assets there is likely to be an absolute threshold of risk minimality. That is to say, since safety plays such a great role in this decision, it does not seem likely that willingness to assume a greater risk plays an important role in explaining SLA growth. If people are more willing to assume risk, other outlets for their funds give ample scope for realization of this shift in their preferences." Marvin Rozen, "Competition among Financial Institutions for Demand and Thrift Deposits," *Journal of Finance*, XVII (May, 1962), 324–25.

[11] See Chart 2.

foreclosure rates, losses on foreclosures, and the reserves available for covering these losses.[12]

Because of stricter regulations and supervision by state and federal agencies, and perhaps to an even greater extent as a result of the prolonged building boom, savings and loan associations have generally experienced comparatively low foreclosure rates during most of the post-1945 period. Although an institution-by-institution analysis is not practical for the purpose of this study, it can be noted that, for members of the Federal Home Loan Bank System (which held almost 88 per cent of all savings and loan association assets at the end of 1945 and over 98 per cent by 1964), average foreclosures on nonfarm residential real estate ranged between 1.7 and 4.6 per 1,000 units annually from 1945 through 1964, with the proportion rising above 2.7 per 1,000 only since 1960. Moreover, although foreclosure rates in some associations are naturally higher than the industry average, it may be assumed that any institution ranging too far above the group average would be brought under more careful supervision and, if necessary, under more stringent control than the others.[13]

[12] The saver rarely concerns himself with these details. In most cases, he simply relies on the fact that his savings are in an organization insured by the FSLIC, the FDIC, or the Massachusetts Deposit Insurance Fund. But because about 30 per cent of the savings and loan associations—with 4 per cent of that industry's assets—are not insured, because state-chartered savings and loan associations and mutual savings banks can drop their insurance provisions, and because a few savers do try to evaluate the quality of their organization's assets, a brief discussion of investments in included above. See pp. 130–32 for a discussion of insurance provisions.

[13] A recent example of the FHLBS's willingness to increase restrictions when rising foreclosure rates indicate that higher net losses might not be far behind occurred in December, 1963. For many months, Joseph R. McMurray, chairman of the FHLBS, had given warnings to those savings and loan associations that were "reaching for high yields [and] risky investments." In October, 1963, noting that corrective steps were not being taken voluntarily, McMurray recommended regulations designed to increase the required reserves of the problem organizations. At the end of December, new and stricter reserve requirements were imposed long before net losses rose anywhere near the point where shareholders' funds were endangered. See the *American Banker*, October 22, 1963, and November 6, 1963.

The foreclosure rates of some savings and loan associations not affiliated with the FHLBS or FSLIC occasionally rise far higher than the averages mentioned above. In some instances these organizations have defaulted and losses have been passed on to savers. But as previously noted, unaffiliated organizations held less than 2 per cent of the industry's assets in 1964.

Actual losses incurred after the resale of foreclosed property have been considerably lower than the foreclosure rates, ranging between 0 and 2.6 per cent of assets from 1945 through 1964.[14] In many instances, thanks to the prolonged building boom, organizations have actually profited from the resale of real estate. Moreover, since 1945, as the next two sections indicate, the net losses of virtually all savings and loan associations have been covered many times over by ready reserves; and by 1964, 96 per cent of all savings accounts were in insured organizations.

Reserves

Although reserves do not in themselves represent cash or create a cash fund, they do indicate the degree of asset loss that can be absorbed without direct jeopardy to the ultimate safety of savings accounts.[15]

There is, of course, no single set of rules for determining precisely when reserves are adequate. Adequacy depends on many factors, some of which are indeterminant—such as the ability of management to evaluate risks and to take the necessary precautions in each investment decision, movements in business and building cycles, and attitudes of investors and savers at any particular time. But if it is assumed that investment conditions in the future will probably be no worse (and most likely a good deal better) than those of the early 1930s, a reserve-to-savings ratio of about 8 per cent would appear sufficient to safeguard savings accounts; this was approximately the level held by mutual savings banks in 1929.[16]

14 Federal Home Loan Bank Board, *Combined Financial Statements,* 1946–64.

15 The term "reserves" as used in this section refers to all general and unallocated reserves, undivided profits, and surplus.

16 The average ratio of general reserves to mutual savings bank deposits was 8.6 per cent in 1929. It must be recalled, however, that this level proved to be adequate largely because mutual savings banks generally received net inflows of savings after they had won the public's confidence by honoring the initial waves of withdrawal requests. The observations above assume that similar conditions would prevail in the future. Concerning these developments it has been noted: "Mutual savings banks contend that losses during the period 1931–44 aggregated 90 per cent of their reserves at the beginning of the period. However, since banks continued to absorb losses out of earnings during this 15-year period, aggregate reserves actually increased from $1,011 million in December 31, 1930, to $1,455

By these standards, data in Table 23 indicate that the average reserve positions of both mutual savings banks and savings and loan associations were probably adequate during the 1945–64 period. And perhaps even more significant, a recent FSLIC ruling requires all members (1) to maintain their reserves at 8 per cent of "risk assets" or (2) to add to reserves according to a predetermined formula before paying interest on savings accounts. Very few member organizations can therefore fall below the desired level for very long.[17]

TABLE 23

Reserve Ratios in the Mutual Savings Bank and Savings and
Loan Association Industries, Selected Years
(*In percentages*)

Year End	Savings and Loan Association Reserves-to-Savings Accounts	Mutual Savings Bank Reserves-to-Savings Deposits
1945	8.7	10.6
1950	9.2	11.4
1955	8.0	10.1
1960	8.0	9.8
1964	7.8	9.0

Sources: National Association of Mutual Savings Banks, *National Fact Book, 1965*, p. 15; United States Savings and Loan League, *Savings and Loan Fact Book, 1965*, p. 106.

Thus, since 1945, the average reserves-to-savings ratio for the savings and loan association industry has been consistently more than three times the size of the largest average loss ratio for any single year.

Supervision and Regulation

Another aspect of the increased safety provided by savings and loan associations is the more stringent supervision and regula-

---

million in December 31, 1944. In no year was there a shrinkage in aggregate reserves of more than $41.2 million, although reserves of individual banks may have declined significantly." George E. Lent, "Comparative Tax Treatment of Mutual Savings Institutions and Commercial Banks," in U.S. Congress, House of Representatives, Committee on Ways and Means, *Tax Revision Compendium*, Vol. 3, 84th Cong., 2d Sess., 1959.

[17] For the details of this regulation see the United States Savings and Loan League, *Savings and Loan Fact Book, 1965*, pp. 96–97.

tion imposed on them since the 1930s by the Federal Home Loan Bank System (FHLBS), the FSLIC, and state chartering agencies. Even to become a member in either the FHLBS or the FSLIC, for example, a savings and loan association first has to meet minimum requirements that in most cases immediately increase the safety of its operations.[18] For instance, each potential member must submit to a complete audit of all its investments, establish and maintain minimum liquidity and reserve levels, provide information about the activities and affiliations of all directors and officers, and produce detailed descriptions of operating procedures, managerial policies, and all past and prospective dealings with savers and borrowers. In every case, appropriate levels of operation must be met and maintained.

Moreover, once a savings and loan association becomes a member of either the FHLBS or the FSLIC, it is required to file monthly financial statements as well as annual reports, to use standard accounting procedures, to be audited at least semi-annually, and to allow an appraisal of its investments at least once a year by an independent agency. In case of any irregularity, additional audits may be made and corrective action taken. Either the FSLIC or the FHLBS has the right to advise any member of any change considered necessary for the protection of savings accounts, and if the suggested revisions are not made voluntarily, fines may be imposed or expulsion may result.

As a result of these and similar provisions, and because insured savings and loan associations have never passed on any losses to depositors, savers have come to rely on the supervisory and regulatory agencies for assurance that complete safety will be maintained at all times. These agencies have undoubtedly "increased the confidence of the public and made many people willing to establish accounts with little prior investigation of the financial standing of particular associations." [19]

[18] A detailed description of the major provisions for the supervision and regulation of both savings and loan associations and mutual savings banks appears in U.S. Congress, House of Representatives, Subcommittee on Domestic Finance, Committee on Banking and Currency, *Comparative Regulations of Financial Institutions*, 88th Cong., 1st Sess., 1963, pp. 65–133.

[19] Harold W. Torgerson, "Developments in Savings and Loan Associations, 1945 to 1953," *Journal of Finance*, IX (September, 1954), 283.

Insurance for Savings Accounts

As noted previously, the well-publicized insurance provisions of savings and loan associations have probably done more than any other single factor to restore public confidence in the safety of savings accounts and to create the impression of equality with mutual savings bank deposits in this respect.[20] Ostensibly the safeguards of the FDIC and the FSLIC are identical; and indeed they are, except with respect to the timing with which funds are returned to savers in case an insured organization defaults.[21] Thus, the FDIC provides:

Whenever an insured bank shall have been closed on account of inability to meet the demands of its depositors, payment of the insured deposits in such bank shall be made by the Corporation as soon as possible . . . either (1) by cash or (2) by making available to each depositor a transferred deposit in a new bank in the same community or in another insured bank in an amount equal to the insured deposit.[22]

And the FSLIC stipulates:

In the event of a default by an insured institution, payment of each insured account in such insured institution which is surrendered and transferred to the Corporation shall be made by the Corporation as soon as possible either (1) by cash or (2) by making available to each insured member a transferred account in a new insured institution in the same community or in another insured institution in an amount equal to the insured account of such insured member.[23]

[20] During the early 1950s, the United States Savings and Loan League took a nationwide, personal interview survey designed to find out how effective its advertising had been in convincing savers that savings and loan association accounts were once again as safe as deposits in competing banking institutions. Its findings appeared to indicate that the efforts had already been significantly successful. The conclusions were summarized by noting: "Virtually all Americans know . . . our accounts were insured by an agency of the Federal Government and there is little evidence that we suffer from a 'depression hangover.'" *Savings and Loan Annals, 1953*, p. 51.

[21] The FSLIC and the FDIC were established by the federal government, and both have the authority (which neither has ever used) to borrow from the U.S. Treasury to meet insurance obligations. They may borrow $750 million and $3 billion, respectively. Even if the current authority proves inadequate, it is hardly conceivable that the federal government would permit either to default on its insurance commitments.

[22] *12 United States Code,* 1821 (f).

[23] *Ibid.,* 1726 (b).

The major substantive difference between these two clauses concerns the words "closed" and "default." With respect to these terms, the FDIC states:

For the purposes of this chapter an insured bank shall be deemed to have been closed on account of inability to meet the demands of its depositors.[24]

And the FSLIC provides:

The term "default" means an adjudication or other official determination of a court of competent jurisdiction or other public authority pursuant to which a conservator, receiver, or other legal custodian is appointed for an insured institution for the purpose of liquidation.[25]

Thus, the laws of the various states require that a mutual savings bank shall be automatically declared closed if it fails to meet its withdrawal requests by the end of the statutory notice period (usually 30–90 days); then the insurance provisions go into effect immediately. But a savings and loan association may adopt a rotation plan for repaying withdrawal requests, and by so doing it may forestall indefinitely the ability of savers to withdraw their funds or to receive compensation from the FSLIC. Only if the directors voluntarily declare their organization in default or if a judgment is brought against the association "through adjudication or other official determination of a court" is a savings and loan association legally defaulted—and only then is the FSLIC obliged to step in and make payments to the holders of savings accounts. It is the procedures necessary to make them effective, therefore, and not the ultimate payment practices that differentiate the insurance provisions of the FSLIC and the FDIC.[26]

Improved performance, more exacting supervision and regulation, and insurance by the FSLIC undoubtedly increased pub-

---

24 *Ibid.*, 1821 (b).

25 *Ibid.*, 1724 (d).

26 In many instances, there is no distinction between either the timing or the payment practices of the FSLIC and the FDIC. In New York, for example, state-chartered savings and loan associations may not invoke a rotation plan. These institutions are automatically declared in default as soon as the 60-day statutory notice period has terminated without withdrawal demands having been honored. In these cases, FSLIC payments to savers begin immediately.

lic confidence in the safety of savings and loan association accounts. But inasmuch as savings and loan associations have never had an advantage over mutual savings banks with respect to safety, shifting attitudes toward the former cannot explain the persistent differences in the growth rates of the two industries during the post-1945 period.

LIQUIDITY SINCE THE FORMATION OF THE FHLBS

As indicated earlier, the inability of many savings and loan associations to meet withdrawal requests upon demand in the early 1930s stemmed largely from the inability of commercial banks to provide the short-term funds upon which they had come to rely. Had emergency cash been available, many associations would not have had to foreclose on their mortgages and to resell property at a loss. Many organizations that failed would probably have been able to provide for a more orderly liquidation of their assets. It was to avoid these and similar problems, as well as to supply long-term funds for home financing, that the FHLBS was formed.[27]

The Federal Home Loan Bank Act was passed in July, 1932. In the words of a FHLBS publication:

(1) The first duty of the [Federal Home Loan] Banks is to provide additional liquidity to the home financing institutions by making advances available to them when an unusual demand for savers' funds occurs. . . .

(2) The second duty . . . is to meet the recurring needs of the members for more loanable funds than the immediate inflow of savings can supply.[28]

[27] Senator Watson, a foremost proponent of the FHLBS, stated: "These [savings and loan] associations have never had a place to go for emergency accommodations or for long-time funds. It is the purpose of this home loan bank bill . . . to function as a reserve system supplying short-time and long-time funds to these institutions." U.S. Congress, Senate, *Senate Report, No. 827,* 72d Cong., 1st Sess., 1932, p. 14.

[28] Federal Home Loan Bank System, *Twentieth Anniversary Booklet, 1952* (Washington, D.C.: Federal Home Loan Bank System, 1952), p. 12. Other agencies such as the Home Owners' Loan Corporation and the Reconstruction Finance Corporation were also formed during the 1930s to help homeowners and home financing institutions with liquidity problems. Most of these were conceived of as emergency organizations, however, whereas the FHLBS was designed to be a permanent institution.

Initially, the FHLBS's resources came from a $125,000,000 sale of stock to the Reconstruction Finance Corporation and from stock purchased by joining organizations. Subsequently, the System received funds from time and demand deposits of members, from retained earnings, and from the sale of its own securities. As a standby precaution, the United States Treasury is permanently authorized to purchase up to one billion dollars of the FHLBS's consolidated obligations. At present no such securities are outstanding.

The eleven regional banks (originally twelve) are authorized to make loans to any affiliated organization up to *50 per cent* of the member's total withdrawable savings balances when the funds are to be used to meet withdrawal demands. Within this limit the regional banks establish a line of credit for each member.[29]

Since its formation, all federally chartered savings and loan associations have been required to join the FHLBS, while affiliation has been optional for state-chartered associations. Membership rose very rapidly immediately after the System was formed (as Table 24 indicates), and by 1935 member organizations held more than half of the savings and loan association industry's assets. This figure climbed to over 87 per cent by 1945, and by 1964 only 1.6 per cent of the industry's assets remained in unaffiliated organizations. To an important extent, these developments helped re-create the impression that at least those savings and loan associations in the FHLBS could once again be relied on to supply liquidity upon demand.[30]

[29] FHLBS policy limits borrowing to an amount up to 17.5 per cent of each member's total withdrawable savings when the advances are to be used for purposes other than meeting withdrawal demands. For additional details about the FHLBS's source and use of funds see United States Savings and Loan League, *Savings and Loan Fact Book, 1965*, pp. 116–21.

[30] Mutual savings banks are also eligible to join the FHLBS, but until recently very few have. Partially this has been due to the fact that they have traditionally provided their own liquidity and therefore have seen little advantage in affiliating with an organization designed primarily to provide still another source of liquid funds. Moreover, many mutual savings bankers were reluctant to join an agency that seemed to be dominated by savings and loan association officials. To make matters even less inviting, dues were figured on the same basis for all members. In effect this would have meant that the comparatively liquid mutual savings banks would have been subsidizing less liquid savings and loan associa-

TABLE 24

Savings and Loan Association Affiliation with the
Federal Home Loan Bank System

Year	Members	Members' Assets (in millions of dollars)	Per Cent of Industry's Assets	Total Advances (in millions of dollars)	Balance Outstanding (in millions of dollars)	Number of Borrowers at Year End
1935	3,455	2,308	56.2	59.1	102.7	2,192
1940	3,824	4,411	76.9	134.2	201.5	2,262
1945	3,658	7,681	87.8	277.7	194.9	916
1950	3,894	15,469	91.6	674.8	816.0	2,279
1955	4,307	36,024	95.7	1,251.7	1,416.8	2,408
1960	4,694	69,330	97.2	1,843.2	1,980.8	2,371
1964	4,985	117,200	98.4	5,563.5	5,324.5	2,795

Source: United States Savings and Loan League, *Savings and Loan Fact Book,
1964,* pp. 112, 117.

The FHLBS's contribution to the restoration of public confidence in the safety of savings and loan associations is indicated
by the fact that, while the industry's assets rose by $3.1 billion
from 1940 through 1945, assets of FHLBS members increased
by $3.3 billion. Thus, not only were virtually all savings placed
into savings and loan associations received by institutions affiliated with the FHLBS, but also many additional organizations
joined the System.

Throughout the 1945–64 period, almost all savings and loan

---

tions. Moreover, in many states, mutual savings banks established their own
funds for emergency and short-term uses.

By the end of 1964, however, 46 mutual savings banks had joined the FHLBS.
Of these, more than two thirds have become members since 1960. For a discus-
sion of advantages and disadvantages to mutual savings banks in joining the
FHLBS, see E. Bruce Fredrickson, "The Federal Home Loan Bank System: Some
Aspects of Savings Bank Membership" (New York: Research Department, Na-
tional Association of Mutual Savings Banks, November, 1961).

The United States Savings and Loan League has observed that mutual savings
bank membership in the FHLBS "is an indication of the converging interests and
growing similarity of mutual savings banks and savings and loan associations.
With a steadily rising percentage of their assets invested in mortgage loans, savings banks are becoming FHLBS members in order to avail themselves of an important additional source of liquidity. Their interest in membership also was
stimulated by the reduction in the FHLBS capital stock purchase requirement
that became effective in 1962." *Savings and Loan Fact Book, 1964,* p. 113.

associations met their savers' withdrawal demands upon request,
and this performance undoubtedly improved the public's confidence in the liquidity of savings accounts and advanced the
industry's growth rates above what they would have been otherwise. By the mid-1950s, the observation that savings and loan
associations no longer suffered from a "depression hangover"
applied as much to liquidity as to safety. Although a few savings
and loan associations have from time to time required notice
periods, the industry's over-all performance indicates that confidence in the ability of all FHLBS members (and almost all
other savings and loan associations as well) to provide liquid
funds upon request continues to be warranted.

Mutual savings banks, on the other hand, honored virtually
all of their withdrawal requests during the 1930s and during all
subsequent years as well.[31] Currently there is every reason to
believe that this fine record will be continued. Throughout the
post-1945 period, therefore—regardless of whether attitudes
toward liquidity are based on past performance, current conditions, or expectations—confidence in mutual savings banks
would always have been greater than or equal to (but never less
than) confidence in savings and loan associations. Nothing in a
comparison of the safety and liquidity of the two types of institutions explains why savings and loan associations grew consistently faster that mutual savings banks since 1945. In fact, inasmuch as confidence in the safety and liquidity of a savings
deposit institution is a *sine qua non* of deposit expansion, the
consistently more rapid growth of savings and loan associations
redirects attention to the importance of differences between their
locations and those of mutual savings banks and to factors conducive to savings deposit growth within the areas being served.

31 For a detailed record of their provisions for liquidity during this period,
see W. H. Steiner, *Mutual Savings Bank Liquidity: A Report to the Committee
on Corporate Securities* (New York: National Association of Mutual Savings
Banks, 1957); August Ihlefeld, "Savings Bank Liquidity," *United States Investor*,
May 2, 1960; Gordon H. Jones and Charles E. Rauch, "Liquidity—What Is Adequate?" *Savings Bank Journal*, August, 1959; J. Brooke Willis, "Gross Flows of
Funds Through Mutual Savings Banks," *Journal of Finance*, XV (May, 1960),
170–90; and National Association of Mutual Savings Banks, *Annual Report:
Facts and Figures, 1964*.

8

Branching and Chartering Limitations on Mutual Savings Banks

THIS CHAPTER EXAMINES two aspects of government legislation and policy with respect to the structure of the mutual savings bank industry, namely, branching and chartering. It is assumed that the public interest is best served when the major goals of government restrictions on the structure of deposit-receiving industries are designed to ensure that savings deposits will be safe and withdrawable upon demand, that fundamentally similar institutions are treated the same, and that competition is encouraged in all ways consistent with the first two standards.[1] It is argued here that under certain conditions mutual savings banks should be provided with broader branching and chartering opportunities.[2]

[1] There are, of course, many other standards currently being used for controlling entry. Most of these, notably the "need" and "convenience" criteria, involve many difficult definitional problems that could be eliminated if the concern for safety and liquidity were handled directly. For a criticism of the "need" and "convenience" criteria, see David Alhadeff, "Reconsideration of Restrictions on Bank Entry," *Quarterly Journal of Economics*, LXXVI (May, 1962), 246–63.

[2] This chapter is concerned with only two of the three major aspects of public control affecting the structure of deposit-receiving industries: controls on branching and chartering. Recent discussions (including bibliographies) of the third subject, mergers, include William Paul Smith, "Measures of Banking Structure and Competition," *Federal Reserve Bulletin*, September, 1965, pp. 1212–22, and Tynan Smith, "Research on Banking Structure and Performance," *Federal Reserve Bulletin*, April, 1966, pp. 488–98. Also see Comptroller of the Currency, U.S. Treasury, *The Banking Structure in Evolution* (Washington, D.C.: Government Printing Office, 1964).

OPPORTUNITIES FOR BRANCHING

Since the end of World War II, the constant migration of people and businesses to suburban areas, population growth, and rising incomes have sharply increased the demand for savings facilities. Accordingly, the incentives for institutions to expand geographically to compete for personal deposits have been substantial.

Since 1945, the primary method for extending financial services into new areas has been the opening of additional branch offices rather than the organization of new institutions (see Table 25). Branch offices are generally easier and less costly to

TABLE 25

Number of Branches of Mutual Savings Banks, Savings and Loan
Associations, and Commercial Banks, 1945 and 1964

	(1) *Number of* *Institutions*	*(2)* *Number of* *Branches*	*(3)* *(2) ÷ (1)*
MSB			
1945	542	143	.26
1964	507	651	1.28
Change	− 35	+ 508	
SLA			
1945	6,149	n.a.	n.a.
1964	6,248	2,664	.43
Change	+ 99	+ 2,664 [a]	
CB			
1945	14,183	4,025	.28
1964	13,760	14,338	1.04
Change	− 423	+ 10,313	

Sources: National Association of Mutual Savings Banks, *National Fact Book, 1965*, p. 4; United States Savings and Loan League, *Savings and Loan Fact Book, 1965*, p. 86; Comptroller of the Currency, U.S. Treasury, *The Banking Structure in Evolution* (Washington, D.C.: Government Printing Office, 1964), p. 21.

[a] Although the number of savings and loan association branches is not available for 1945, data for subsequent years indicate that there were very few. Thus the change from 1945 through 1964 is close to the number at the end of the period.

n.a. = Not available.

start, safer and more economical to operate, and less difficult to get chartered. In conjunction with their parent organizations, moreover, branches are more efficient with respect to utilizing investment alternatives, surpluses, and earnings, and also are often better able to provide competent management and managerial succession. They are, therefore, usually more able to withstand the costs and competition frequently associated with opening a new location.[3]

Despite the advantages of branching and the changing demands for deposit facilities, most states impose limitations on the formation, number, and location of branch offices—limitations that have no direct connection with the safety or liquidity of the institutions involved. Moreover, in all states with both savings and loan associations and mutual savings banks, different limitations are imposed on the two types of institutions. Savings and loan associations are consistently favored in one or both of the following ways: by branching and locating opportunities that are directly and obviously unequal and by the advantages inherent in the fact that savings and loan associations have a dual chartering system while mutual savings banks do not.

LIMITATIONS ON BRANCHING

Considerable diversity exists between the branching opportunities of mutual savings banks and savings and loan associations in the eighteen mutual savings bank states. In all except Wisconsin, New Hampshire, Vermont, and Delaware, opportunities for savings and loan associations to branch are greater in at least one of four ways: [4]

[3] For a discussion of the advantages of branching versus new chartering, see Jules I. Bogen, "Branch Banking for Mutual Savings Banks," in Jules I. Bogen, ed., *Economic Study of Savings Banking in New York State* (New York: Savings Banks Association of New York, 1956), pp. 65–86.

[4] In Wisconsin, statutes prohibit either industry from opening branches; in New Hampshire and Vermont, the absence of statutory provisions has been interpreted as prohibiting branching for both groups—although as a result of mergers there is one mutual savings bank branch in each state; in Delaware, mutual savings banks have been allowed to open six branches while savings and loan associations have none.

For a summary of the laws of the various mutual savings bank states, see

1) In four states—Indiana, Minnesota, Ohio, and Oregon—the absence of statutory branching provisions has been interpreted as permissive for savings and loan associations and prohibitive for mutual savings banks. Thus, mutual savings banks in these states have two branches (as a result of mergers) and savings and loan associations have 405.

2) In at least five states—Maryland, New Jersey, Pennsylvania, Connecticut, and Massachusetts—branching is limited primarily to home office communities and in only a few cases to contiguous counties as well. Thus, savings and loan associations, being more often situated in suburban areas, have greater opportunity than mutual savings banks to further increase the number of their suburban locations.

3) In some states—notably New York—the differences are even more explicit, as discussed below. And, of course, with almost 60 per cent of all mutual savings bank deposits in New York, the situation there is of considerable importance.

4) Finally, in all states that permit branching, the dual chartering system makes it possible for savings and loan associations to apply leverage on either the state or federal chartering agency in order to obtain a specific branching location, while mutual savings banks must accept and live with the decisions of their respective state agencies.

In New York

Revisions of the New York Banking Law in 1946 established regulations governing the branching of mutual savings banks and savings and loan associations. Under these revisions, which were effective until 1960, mutual savings banks in cities and towns of less than 30,000 were prohibited from maintaining branches. Institutions in cities between 30,000 and 250,000 were allowed to have one branch; two branches were permitted

---

"Branch Laws for Savings Banks Strike Multitude of Dissonant Chords," *Savings Bank Journal*, XLVIII, No. 12 (February, 1963), 20–23. For a detailed state-by-state study of branch statutes for both mutual savings banks and savings and loan associations, see Jean Gills Harth, "Branch Statutes of State Financing Institutions," *Legal Bulletin of the United States Savings and Loan League*, March, 1958), pp. 33–101.

in cities between 250,000 and 1,000,000; and up to three were authorized in cities with populations over 1,000,000. In all instances, the branches had to be *within the same city or borough in which the principal office was located.*

Savings and loan associations, on the other hand, could have only one branch (in addition to those resulting from mergers or from conversion of a savings "station" into a branch office). However, opportunities for locating in suburban areas were considerably more liberal than for mutual savings banks. First, any association eligible to branch could open its additional office *anywhere within a 50-mile radius of the home office.* Thus, even institutions in the state's largest urban areas were able to move into and preempt many of the best suburban locations, while mutual savings banks remained locked into their home office cities—and in some cases into home boroughs. In addition, all savings and loan associations in towns of 20,000 and over were permitted to maintain a branch (as opposed to a minimum population of 30,000 for mutual savings banks). This was yet another opportunity for savings and loan associations to preempt choice suburban locations before the population was large enough to permit mutual savings bank branching. Moreover, although the Federal Home Loan Bank Board follows state regulations with respect to the maximum number of branches it will authorize for a federally-chartered savings and loan association, in practice, as discussed below, the mere existence of a dual chartering system frequently results in treatment that is more liberal for savings and loan associations than for mutual savings banks.

In 1960 the New York legislature passed an Omnibus Banking Act which liberalized branching opportunities for both types of institutions.[5] As Table 26 indicates, however, treatment for the two industries continued to be unequal. In addition to differences that can be observed from the table, every savings and loan association continued to be allowed to open one of its branches in a location *up to 50 miles from its home office,* while almost all mutual savings bank branches remained

[5] The law was reenacted in 1961 after its invalidation by the New York Supreme Court on procedural grounds.

confined to the same city or borough as the principal location. The only exceptions were that mutual savings banks in cities between 100,000 and 1,000,000 people were permitted to open one branch within the home county but not over *five miles* from the principal office. And under certain conditions, mutual savings banks and savings and loan associations in New York City could maintain one branch in parts of Nassau and Westchester counties, and both types of institutions in Nassau and Westchester could have up to two additional branches, one of which might be in New York City. While these exceptions left intact many of the differences between the branching opportunities of the two groups, the 1960 Omnibus Banking Act did represent an important breakthrough in allowing mutual savings banks to branch in suburbs, albeit under highly restrictive conditions. And, as previously noted, the branches opened in suburban communities pursuant to the 1960 Act contributed significantly to the growth of mutual savings banking throughout the state.[6]

In addition to the other restrictions, mutual savings banks and savings and loan associations are confined by "home protection" clauses that prohibit the opening of branches in any city or village with a population of one million or less in which is located "the principal office of a bank, trust company, or national banking association" or where there is already the head office of "another mutual savings bank," or in the case of savings and loan associations where there is already "another savings and loan association." Despite the similarities of these home

---

[6] The Omnibus Banking Act of 1960 also opened parts of Nassau and Westchester counties to New York City commercial banks under certain conditions. After examining the results of this action with respect to Nassau County, a recent study concludes that the broader branching opportunities improved services to the public: "The considerable expansion of banking facilities in [Nassau County] reflected not only a response of banking investment to more than a decade of unusual growth in population, income, and industry, but also cognizance by the regulatory agencies of the need for satisfying new demands for banking services through appropriate entry policies. . . . The performance of the system from the standpoint of its customers has materially improved in a number of dimensions in recent years." David C. Motter and Deane Carson, "Bank Entry and the Public Interest: A Case Study," *National Banking Review*, I, No. 4 (June, 1964), 511–12.

protection clauses, their effects have fallen more heavily on mutual savings banks than on savings and loan associations because a greater number of the locations that would have otherwise been open to mutual savings banks have been closed.[7] In addition, savings and loan associations are permitted to enter many more areas with small populations, and these are the regions that generally have fewer principal offices of other banking institutions. As late as 1965, the Superintendent of Banking observed:

According to the most recent figures of the State Banking Department there exist today 86 unexercised savings banks privileges, of which 74 may be used only within New York City, Nassau, and Westchester. The 12 remaining branch privileges may be exercised, subject to certain geographic limitations, by individual savings banks in [10 upstate counties]. State-chartered savings and loan associations, on the other hand, have a total of 236 unexercised branch privileges, only 76 of which would have to be exercised if at all, within the New York City metropolitan area.[8]

Important new amendments to the New York Banking Law became effective on May 10, 1966. Many of these once again changed the branching opportunities of mutual savings banks and savings and loan associations, eliminating the numerical inequalities that previously existed. (See Table 26.) However, the restrictions of home protection clauses continued to fall more heavily on mutual savings banks, and in at least one respect the inequality was increased.[9] In addition, almost every savings and

7 A critical analysis of the current "home protection" regulations as they apply to mutual savings banks appears in Eugene M. Lerner, "An Analysis of Home Office Protection," in State of New York, *Legislative Document No. 14*, March 15, 1963), pp. 52–57.

8 Frank Wille, Superintendent of Banks, "Statement before the Joint Legislative Committee to Revise the Banking Law," December 6, 1965, quoted in Savings Bank Association of New York State, *Benefits for the Public . . . from Expanded Savings Bank Services in New York State* (New York: Savings Bank Association of New York State, 1965), p. 31.

9 The home protection rules as amended in 1966 excluded mutual savings bank branches from "any city or village with a population of *one million or less* in which is located the principal office of a bank, trust company, or national banking association . . . [or] another savings bank." A similar ruling was applied to savings and loan associations, but only with respect to towns and cities of "less than thirty thousand." *New York Laws of 1966*, Ch. 324, par. 17, sec. 2(c)

TABLE 26

Branch Offices Permitted Mutual Savings Banks and Savings and Loan
Associations under the Omnibus Banking Acts of 1960 and 1966

	Number of Branches Permitted Mutual Savings Banks		Number of Branches Permitted Savings and Loan Associations	
Population	1960	1966	1960	1966
0– 30,000	0	1	1	1
30,000– 100,000	1	2	2	2
100,000– 200,000	2	3	2	3
200,000–1,000,000	3	4	3	4
1,000,000 and over	4	7	4	7

Sources: Data for 1960 are from the *New York Banking Law*, Art. VI, sec. 240,
Art. X, sec. 396. Figures for 1966 appear in Chapter 324 of the New York Banking Laws.

loan association retained the opportunity to locate one branch
up to 50 miles from the principal office. Also under the new
amendments, all branches permitted to mutual savings banks in
cities over 1,000,000—New York City and Buffalo—were required
to be within the city limits, except under the few circumstances
noted above. Thus, mutual savings banks in New York City—
which hold about 45 per cent of the industry's deposits—continue
to be confined almost entirely to a region that already has more
deposit institutions per square mile than any other city in the
world. Finally, of course, savings and loan associations have re-
course to a dual chartering system, while mutual savings banks
have nowhere to turn if their branching applications are turned
down.[10]

and par. 18, sec. 2(h). For the details of the 1966 amendments, see all of
chapter 324.

[10] Perhaps the best example of the benefits of a dual chartering system is the
fact that the amendments of 1966 were passed. Prior to this, there had been
widespread concern that, unless opportunities for state-chartered commercial
banks were brought into closer line with the opportunities of federally-chartered commercial banks, many of the former would convert to federal charters,
following the example set earlier that year by the Chase Manhattan Bank.
Broader branching and investment opportunities for mutual savings banks and
savings and loan associations were necessary to muster the support needed for
passage of the more liberal commercial bank legislation. As it was, the amendments passed the state Assembly by only one vote.

Suggestions for Change in Branching Regulations

Many of the attitudes underlying current limitations on the branching opportunities of mutual savings banks in the United States date back to days when transportation and communication over any distance required arduous trips by horseback and stagecoach. There were likely to be few advantages and many costs in maintaining distant branch offices. However, when mutual savings banks were first organized there was little need for branches; when sufficient demand for additional savings facilities developed, new banks were started. Reflecting these facts, many states did not permit mutual savings banks to open branches until well into the twentieth century, and even then the number and the regions in which they could be located were severely restricted. Communication between the main office and the branches would have been difficult under any circumstances, and it is possible that these limitations were considered necessary for the protection of depositors.

Today, however, with high-speed transportation and communication making it thoroughly feasible for trustees and administrators in the home office to be fully and constantly apprised of conditions in distant branches, these limitations are no longer needed for the safety or liquidity of deposits. With population shifting without regard to political boundaries and with mutual savings banks—the group with the best record for safety and liquidity among all types of deposit institutions— being the most restricted, there is clearly a need to reevaluate the current branching laws.

The safety and liquidity problems that entry restrictions were originally designed to prevent are currently being met by direct regulation and supervision of operations, periodic examination of financial records, requirements concerning reserves and surpluses, standards for the activities of management, and the widespread use of deposit insurance.[11] Since these and other

[11] With respect to commercial banks, it has been noted that "to prevent entry by persons who might ignore the public trust, [government chartering agencies] carefully evaluate the background, character, and competence of the organizers and prospective management; to enhance the safety of the bank and to protect depositors, they set minimum capital requirements; to control certain

controls are presumably considered sufficient to assure the safety and liquidity of deposits, the public interest would not be injured by foregoing the indirect, additional, and haphazard protection provided by entry barriers. If the direct controls are considered insufficient, they should be tightened.

In addition to duplicating efforts unnecessarily, current branching legislation often fails to provide basically similar institutions with similar opportunities. In states like New York the discrepancies with respect to mutual savings banks and savings and loan associations are obvious. To do away with these as well as many of the more subtle forms of discrimination and to encourage the maximum competition consistent with appropriate standards for safety and liquidity, both groups should be permitted to open an unlimited number of branches on a statewide basis whenever the direct regulations for safeguarding deposits are met.[12] States that currently allow statewide branching provide ample testimony to the fact that this can be thoroughly consistent with the safety and liquidity of savings.

---

specific abuses, they regulate particular actions (e.g., loans to officers) ; and, to assure that the bank is prudently and conservatively managed and conforms to high banking standards, they constantly supervise and examine bank operations. *Regardless of entry requirements, direct regulation of this sort is necessary* to provide effective protection against abuses." Alhadeff, "Reconsideration . . .", pp. 248–49 (emphasis added).

This is also true with respect to all other deposit-receiving institutions. Many aspects of direct regulation and supervision of savings and loan associations and mutual savings banks are discussed in chapter 7.

[12] This suggestion, although not so broad in scope, is similar to one made recently by the President's Committee on Financial Institutions. The Committee, which had already recommended that mutual savings banks be given federal charters, also recommended that national commercial banks, federally-chartered savings and loan associations, and federally-chartered mutual savings banks be permitted "to establish branches within 'trading areas' irrespective of State laws, and State laws should be revised to provide corresponding privileges to state-chartered banks." Committee on Financial Institutions, *Report of the Committee on Financial Institutions to the President of the United States"* (Washington, D.C.: Government Printing Office, 1963), pp. 47, 52.

The Committee used the definition of "trading area" provided by the Commission on Money and Credit, namely, "[a] geographic area that embraces the natural flow of trade from an outlying geographical territory to and from a metropolitan center. It may be state-wide, less than state-wide, or more than state-wide. The test of drawing boundaries should be delegated to an appropriate governmental agency as was done in establishing the Federal Reserve districts." Commission on Money and Credit, *Money and Credit: Their Influence on Jobs, Prices, and Growth* (Englewood Cliffs, N.J.: Prentice-Hall, 1961), p. 166.

Even though opening new areas for branching and equalizing branching opportunities for mutual savings banks and savings and loan associations would bring the benefits of increased competition to many additional regions, it is unlikely that many states will take the necessary action in the foreseeable future. To a large extent, this is a political rather than an economic problem. Many suburban institutions have a vested interest in perpetuating restrictions that currently protect them from increased competition. This is particularly true of commercial banks, although in a few cases suburban savings and loan associations and even suburban mutual savings banks have also fought the liberalization of mutual savings bank branching opportunities.[13]

POTENTIAL ADVANTAGES OF FEDERAL CHARTERS

Mutual savings bankers might easily have organized a dual chartering system during the 1930s, but their unparalleled record of safety and liquidity led many of them to conclude that federal charters were unnecessary to the successful performance of their services. The disadvantages of being regulated and supervised by a federal agency seemed on balance to outweigh the advantages of federal charters. On the other hand, savings and loan associations, commercial banks, and credit unions—thousands of which failed during the depression—welcomed the opportunities afforded by dual chartering systems to increase their efficiency and to help restore their public images as responsible deposit-receiving institutions.

Since the end of World War II, however, competitive relationships among financial institutions have changed so dramatically that many mutual savings bankers now see significant ad-

[13] For the standard commercial bank arguments against broader branching opportunities for mutual savings banks, see the New York State Bankers Association, *Banks and the Future of New York State* (New York: New York State Bankers Association, 1964). Perhaps banking legislation that provides benefits to all major types of financial institutions—such as the Omnibus Banking Act which recently passed the Senate and Assembly in New York—will prove to be the only way to broaden and equalize the branching opportunities for mutual savings banks and savings and loan associations.

vantages in having a dual chartering system. As long as adoption of federal charters would be permissive rather than mandatory, establishment of a dual chartering system for mutual savings banks would be consistent with the three objectives accepted by this study as appropriate for government regulation of financial institutions.[14] Such a system, moreover, could be established at virtually no cost to the public.

The ideal federal chartering system for mutual savings banks should permit conversions between state and federal charters as well as between federally-chartered mutual savings banks and federally-chartered savings and loan associations. In all cases, standards could be maintained to ensure the constant safety and liquidity of deposits. Furthermore, an institution affiliated with either the FDIC or the FSLIC should be permitted to move from one agency to the other, together with its share of the insurance corporation's surplus account.[15]

Among the developments that this type of chartering system would make possible are:

1. the organization *de novo* of mutual savings banks in the thirty-two states where none may be chartered at present;

2. conversion of mutual savings banks between state and federal charters;

3. conversion between savings and loan associations and mutual savings banks; and

4. competition between chartering agencies.

The following pages discuss a few aspects of these possibilities.

Organization de novo

Only three mutual savings banks have been organized *de novo* in the past thirty years, while more than 140 federally-chartered savings and loan associations have been formed in the past five years alone. There are at least three reasons for the almost complete lack of interest in founding new mutual sav-

---

14 See p. 136.

15 Not all of these suggestions are included in the current federal chartering bill. For a detailed analysis of a bill similar to the one that is currently being proposed, see U.S. Congress, House of Representatives, *Federal Charter Legislation for Mutual Savings Banks, H.R. 258,* 88th Cong., 1st Sess., 1963.

ings banks, and none of these would be removed by the introduction of federal chartering.

First, there is no personal profit incentive to form a mutual
savings bank. Founders and trustees receive no salaries, and,
traditionally, prohibitions against special privileges and self-
dealing have been broadly interpreted and strictly enforced.
Founders and directors of savings and loan associations, on the
other hand, may receive salaries and may profit from positions
or financial interests in real estate companies, law firms, contract-
ing organizations, insurance companies, and other organizations
that receive business from the institutions with which they are
affiliated. Thus, persons interested in seeing their community
provided with additional deposit facilities or an increased supply of mortgage funds would be most likely to organize a savings
and loan association in preference to a mutual savings bank
even if federal chartering for the latter were to become
available.

Secondly, FDIC membership is mandatory for mutual savings
banks in most states, and the initial capital fund required by the
FDIC for the approval of new membership has usually been
large.[16] On the other hand, not all savings and loan associations
have to be insured, and capital funds required of those that
have sought affiliation with the FSLIC have been substantially
lower than those established by the FDIC.[17] More permissive
capital requirements need not jeopardize the safety or liquidity
of mutual savings bank deposits, since they do not appear to
have done so for savings and loan associations. Unless a federal

[16] In general terms, the FDIC procedure for setting minimum capital requirements consists of computing the average reserve-to-asset ratio for the mutual
savings bank industry (currently about 8 per cent), projecting the deposits
anticipated at the end of the proposed organization's first three years, and
requiring a fund that would be 8 per cent of the expected amount. Obviously,
these amounts reach giant proportions in areas with large populations or
potentially rapid growth—the very regions in which it would be most desirable
to start a mutual savings bank.

[17] The FSLIC and the Federal Home Loan Bank System have recently followed the policy of requiring initial capital funds to be equal to 10 per cent
of the savings accounts subscribed to *prior to the opening* of a new organization.
Reserves must be added as the institution grows, but these, of course, can come
from retained earnings.

chartering bill allows mutual savings banks to affiliate with the FSLIC, or unless the FDIC lowers its initial capital requirements, it is unlikely that many mutual savings banks will be formed *de novo* even if the bill is passed.

A third factor is a product of the first two: namely, there are costs and risks, for which there are no monetary compensations, in starting a mutual savings bank. The initial capital fund, for example, is usually composed of subordinate debentures. This fund is nonwithdrawable; it can be returned only after the organization has generated the required surplus out of earnings—and sometimes this takes years. In case of termination, the fund can be returned only after all other obligations, including deposits, are paid. Founders may also be *required* to put up additional capital any time regulatory agencies determine that supplementary funds are necessary for the safety of operations. Yet interest rates on the initial capital are typically no higher than on regular deposits.

With savings and loan associations, on the other hand, the initial fund may be withdrawn after five years, or in as little as three years if reserves have reached 3 per cent of net assets. Interest rates on this capital are usually higher than those on regular savings accounts.

These observations do not preclude the possibility that a few mutual savings banks might be formed *de novo* if federal charters become available. Some people may feel strongly about organizing this type of institution, and with the possibility of receiving part of the initial capital from trade organizations, at least a few new mutual savings banks may be founded. This type of help was given mutual savings banks formed *de novo* in Alaska in 1962 and in Rockland County, New York, in 1965. Under the legislation as currently proposed, however, it is unlikely that there will be a large number of newly organized mutual savings banks.

Choice Between State and Federal Charters

Savings and loan associations, commerical banks, and credit unions currently have the freedom to convert between state and federal charters, and the ideal federal chartering bill would give mutual savings banks the same opportunity. Assuming that federal standards would be as high as those of the various states, this would not only create a more equitable situation with no detrimental effect on the safety and liquidity of mutual savings bank deposits but would also introduce an element of choice by permitting each mutual savings bank to move to the type of charter that appeared most consistent with its needs and objectives.

Unlike the possibility for the formation *de novo* of mutual savings banks, opportunity for conversion between state and federal charters would probably result in a substantial amount of activity. Many mutual savings bankers feel that there is economic value in having the word "federal" in their institution's title; others would be attracted by opportunities that would probably become available to federally-chartered, but not to state-chartered, institutions—such as the right to participate in mortgage loans with other federally-chartered organizations. Moreover, federal chartering would allow a mutual savings bank to move out from under the control of a state chartering agency dominated by financial institutions unfriendly to the expansion of mutual savings banking. And, of course, there would always be the possibility of returning to a state charter if the state agency developed advantages that could not be obtained at the federal level.

Conversion Between Savings and Loan Associations and Mutual Savings Banks

The ideal federal chartering act would also permit conversions between federal mutual savings banks and federal savings and loan associations. At least a few savings and loan association directors have indicated an interest in seeing their institutions converted to mutual savings banks, if this option becomes available.[18]

18 For example, see A. D. Theobald, *Partners in Progress,* address at the 16th Midyear Meeting of the National Association of Mutual Savings Banks, December 2, 1962, p. 19. Also see statements by Messrs. Courshon, Bliss, Fletcher, and Hoeft in *Federal Charter Legislation for Mutual Savings Banks.*

The two reasons most frequently given for desiring the change are that mutual savings banks have broader investment powers and that there is prestige and economic value in having the word "bank" in a title. Many savings and loan association officials already conceive of their institutions as being more like mutual savings banks than like the traditional savings and loan associations, and at least a few feel that the inability to convert prevents them from achieving a degree of efficiency.

Competition Between Chartering Agencies

A dual chartering system for mutual savings banks would not only provide an opportunity for relief from arbitrary or unduly restrictive regulations but would also bring to that industry many of the advantages of competition between chartering agencies. As one state banking commissioner has observed:

One of the great benefits of the dual chartering system is the effort which is generated on the part of both segments to improve their banking laws and procedures so as to attract banks to their segments. Any improvement in one segment generates an inducement to improvement in the other.[19]

Moreover, the diffusion of authority is not generally seen as an inefficient duplication of resources but rather, as yet another state banking superintendent has noted, as an "opportunity for developing and testing new practices under relatively controlled circumstances." [20]

Although the advantages of competition between chartering agencies cannot be precisely measured, the following quotations are offered as evidence that both savings and loan officials and commercial bankers recognize and make use of the leverage that such arrangements provide for their industries.

A recent publication written for the United States Savings and Loan League claims:

[19] Randolph Hughes, testimony before the House Banking and Currency Committee, quoted in the *American Banker,* May 6, 1963, p. 1.

[20] Oren Root, "Memo From: Oren Root," *New York State Banking,* I, No. 2 (June, 1963), 9.

The dual system of charters has an advantage from the viewpoint of checks and balances. Federal regulatory agencies and various state agencies seem to a degree to compete with each other. Individual institutions thus have some ability at times *to play one chartering agency against another* and to introduce innovations into their operations more readily than they would if only a single chartering system existed.[21]

And an officer of the American Bankers Association notes:

It must be recognized that the ability of [commercial] banks to shift from one [chartering] system to the other has certain very definite advantages. Supervisory procedures can become oppressive and harmful, to the point where banks cannot adequately meet the needs of their communities. By maintaining a choice of systems, dual banking not only provides a safety valve for commercial banks but also, and more important, assures that such oppressive supervisory procedures cannot long continue.[22]

The costs of maintaining a dual chartering system are borne almost entirely by affiliated organizations, while the benefits to the public in terms of the improvement in the safety and liquidity of savings and loan associations, commercial banks, and credit unions since the advent of federal chartering have been substantial. In addition, competition between chartering agencies may result in greater incentive for innovation and improvement of supervisory and regulatory techniques, while the dangers of carrying rivalry too far are limited by the fact that no chartering agency can tolerate more than a very few defaults among its membership. Even in such cases, moreover, deposit insurance provides the ultimate safeguard. Of all deposit-receiving industries, only mutual savings banks are without a dual chartering system.

The strongest opposition to federal chartering for mutual savings banks comes from commercial bankers, presumably because of the increased competition they would face if it were

[21] Leon T. Kendall, *The Savings and Loan Business* (Englewood Cliffs, N.J.: Prentice-Hall, 1962), p. 29 (emphasis added).

[22] Charles E. Walker, "The Dual Banking System—Its Strengths and Weaknesses," Address before the annual convention of the Financial Public Relations Association, Atlantic City, N.J., October 15, 1962.

granted. Thus, from the standpoint of achieving federal chartering for mutual savings banks, the arithmetic of political geog-
raphy is harsh indeed. The eighteen states that currently permit
mutual savings banking have a delegate strength in the House of
Representatives of 180 members, not all of whom would necessarily vote for a federal chartering bill. Even if all of these sup-
ported federal chartering, however, 40 other lawmakers from
states that have no mutual savings banking would have to vote
for the bill to build a majority. With eighteen states permitting
mutual savings banks—opposed to thirty-two states that don't—
the outlook in the Senate is even less bright.[23]

However, this does not alter the essential merits of federal
chartering for mutual savings banks: as proposed in this chapter,
the safety and liquidity of mutual savings bank deposits would
continue to be thoroughly supervised and safeguarded, similar
treatment would be provided for similar institutions, and increased competition would be encouraged at virtually no public
expense.

OUTLOOK UNDER PRESENT LIMITATIONS

Competitive pressures are forcing all types of deposit-receiving
institutions to search for and develop new savings and investment services. Compartmental lines are being blurred as organizations try to enter fields that have proved profitable for their

[23] This political situation changed substantially in 1967, when the United
States Savings and Loan League, which had previously strongly opposed federal
charters for mutual savings banks, joined the National Association of Mutual
Savings Banks in support of a compromise bill (H.R. 13118) which would grant
federal charters to mutual savings banks and broader investment opportunities
to savings and loan associations. For a statement of the earlier United States
Savings and Loan League position against federal chartering for mutual savings
banks, see Norman Strunk, "A Federal System of Mutual Savings Banks?"
Savings and Loan News, LXXXVI, No. 5 (May, 1963), 36–52. Typical arguments
against the bill from the commercial banker's point of view appear in statements
by Jack T. Conn on behalf of The American Bankers Association before the
Subcommittee on Bank Supervision and Insurance of the House Banking and
Currency Committee on H.R. 10745, July 18, 1967, and by Lewellyn A. Jennings
on behalf of The American Bankers Association before the House Banking and
Currency Committee on H.R. 13718, November 17, 1967.

rivals. Pressures on mutual savings banks are particularly great because of the limited opportunities they have for geographical expansion. Since they are located primarily in large northeastern cities, where population is declining and where average personal income is rising less rapidly than in suburban and other nonurban regions, unfavorable comparisons between their growth rates and those of savings and loan associations are likely to continue. Furthermore, there is a real possibility of a long-run decline in the number of mutual savings bank deposits.

If they remain confined to their present locations, therefore, mutual savings bankers must be prepared either to face some further deterioration in their competitive position or to intensify their efforts to develop services that can be marketed profitably in urban centers. The first alternative is neither necessary nor realistic. Once deterioration begins, it becomes more and more of a problem to attract talented management, to maintain efficiency, and, in short, to develop the properties necessary for reversing the trend. Furthermore, because most mutual savings banks operate under conditions of falling average costs, any reduction in absolute size would make effective competition even more difficult. And, of course, rival institutions stand ready to provide the desired services and thereby to achieve the economies necessary for enhancing their positions still further at mutual savings bank expense. Mutual savings banks must therefore proceed on two fronts: while trying to increase their opportunities for geographic expansion, they must try to develop the widest possible range of savings and investment services. These efforts are already under way, of course, and they are destined to continue as competitive pressures mount.

To make traditional deposit services more attractive, mutual savings banks in states with ceilings on the amount that can be held in each account are trying to have the maximums increased. In some states, a central distribution service is dividing accounts among many institutions so that large amounts can be fully insured. Thought might also be given to the possibility of accepting large accounts from foreign governments or nonprofit international agencies. These could also be distributed by a central agency. In New York, with 126 mutual savings banks permitted to hold up to $25,000 per account, for example, as much as $3,150,000 could be accepted from one depositor; or if the deposits were from nonprofit organizations there would be no limit to the amount that could be accepted.

School and Christmas savings deposits have, of course, been mutual savings bank services for many years. New types of regular and special accounts might also be considered, with the payment of different interest rates for different types of deposits. Operations could also be improved by the further development of savings instruments that would *not* be withdrawable upon demand. Such deposits would enable these institutions to attract funds from a margin of interest-sensitive investors at premium rates without requiring an across-the-board increase in the interest rates on all deposits. In addition, special accounts might be set up that would permit withdrawals by "bill paying" drafts. Money transfer services might be developed and checking accounts—such as those now offered by a few mutual savings banks in New Jersey, Indiana, Maryland—might be considered for broader use. These and similar services would naturally move the functions of mutual savings banks closer to those of commercial banks.

Mutual savings banks could also move further into nondeposit savings services. In New York, Massachusetts, and Connecticut, Savings Bank Life Insurance is already being sold over the counter to individuals and specific types of groups. This service could be offered in other states as well; perhaps it could be advertised more broadly—conceivably by direct mail—in states where it is presently sold.

Another possibility for expansion is the over-the-counter sale of mutual funds. Although this idea was recently rejected by a group of mutual savings bankers in New York, it is clearly consistent with the mutual savings bank philosophy of serving people of modest means. Services of this type would move the functions of mutual savings banks closer to those of insurance companies, pension funds, and mutual funds.

As they try to become "full service" or "family service" institutions, mutual savings banks must continue to make an effort to expand their lending as well as their savings services. The most natural extension, one that mutual savings bankers have been trying to get permission to develop for many years, is in personal or consumer lending. While trying to obtain more permissive legislation for this service, mutual savings bankers should constantly make full use of their present powers. They can, for example, encourage people to take increased advantage of the possibility of refinancing their mortgages to raise money for nonrealty debts. Even now, many homeowners use the equity in their property as collateral for funds to finance items such as travel, autos and boats, business ventures, stock purchases, or the consolidation of short-term debts. Once again, however, their locations in major urban centers place mutual savings banks at a disadvantage in relation to savings and loan associations. Comparatively few people in urban areas own their homes; thus mutual savings banks are hampered to a greater extent than their more widely dispersed competitors in efforts to develop this profitable lending service.

All states currently allow mutual savings banks to make pass-book loans and many also permit them to make personal loans on the basis of eligible collateral such as life insurance policies. Some states authorize co-maker and character loans, while Delaware and Maryland permit consumer loans if they are "prudent" and "on good security." [24] This type of credit—and perhaps also the recent ruling allowing almost all mutual savings banks to invest up to 5 per cent of their assets in education loans—may serve as precedents for further expansion in the area of personal lending.

Meanwhile, mutual savings banks continue making loans for the construction, purchase, and repair of private homes as well as on a broad range of commercial, industrial, and community properties. They could try to extend these investment opportunities geographically. The 1966 amendments to the New York

[24] A summary of the statutory authority for mutual savings banks in the various states to make personal loans appears in Bogen, *Economic Study*, p. 131.

Banking Law that increase to 20 per cent of assets the amount that mutual savings banks can invest in out of-state conventional mortgages illustrate one of the ways that the services of these institutions can be expanded and competition with local lending institutions increased. In addition, they could try to make their investments more attractive for resale by grouping together mortgages of varying risks, and then—at a premium that would cover costs and possible losses—offer a risk-free package to pension and trust funds. If mutual savings bankers found that they could profitably invest even more funds than those available from net deposit flows, the sale of debentures might also be considered. This would always be a limited but at times probably a very useful source of funds.

Among other investments, mutual savings banks could profitably increase their long-term holdings of corporate securities. In New York, for example, the banking law was changed in 1965 to allow these institutions to invest up to 7.5 per cent of their assets in corporate stocks; currently the industry average is only 1.9 per cent in that state. Greater purchases of corporate securities would diversify still further the lending services of these institutions.

Thus, competitive pressures that once moved the functions of mutual savings banks and savings and loan associations along convergent lines are now forcing mutual savings banks to search for and develop new services, many of which are similar to those of rival industries. This is a continuing part of a larger process in which all types of deposit-receiving institutions are trying to diversify their services, suggesting that ultimately these institutions may become similar multiservice organizations.

But the development of mutual savings banks into multiservice financial centers has not yet taken place, and, if current conditions persist, it is entirely possible that such progress may be thwarted indefinitely by existing legislative restrictions. Thus, while the effort is being made to broaden their opportunities for developing additional services, it is essential to the growth of mutual savings banks that they be given the broadest possible opportunities—consistent with adequate provisions for the safety and liquidity of deposits—to offer their services in regions where demand is growing most rapidly. If legislative restrictions continue to keep mutual savings banks from expanding geographically and also from developing and offering new services, their ability to respond safely and competitively to current and future savings needs will be seriously and unnecessarily impaired.

Appendix A: Growth of Mutual Savings Banks and Savings and Loan Associations, Selected Regions, 1945–1964

APPENDIX CHART 1
Gross Savings in Mutual Savings Banks and Savings and
Loan Associations in Mutual Savings
Bank States, 1945–1964

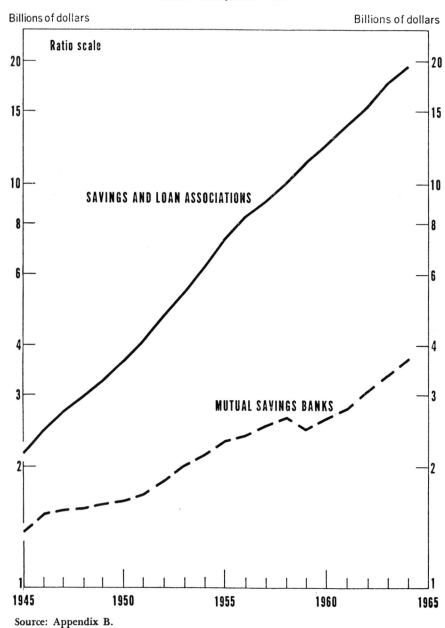

Source: Appendix B.

APPENDIX CHART 2
Spreads Between the Average Annual Net Growth Rates
of Savings and Loan Associations and Mutual
Savings Banks in Mutual Savings
Bank States, 1946–1964

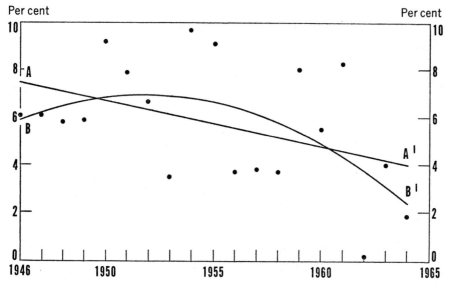

Source: Appendix B.
Note: The equation for line AA', with its standard error and coefficient of correlation, is:

$$SLA_{growth\ rate} - MSB_{growth\ rate} = 7.72 - .19x \qquad R^2 = .21$$
$$(.10)$$

The comparable data for BB' are:

$$SLA_{growth\ rate} - MSB_{growth\ rate} = 5.56 + .42x - .04x^2 \qquad R^2 = .31$$
$$(.28) \quad (.01)$$

APPENDIX CHART 3
Gross Savings in Savings and Loan Associations and Mutual Savings Banks in New York, 1946–1964

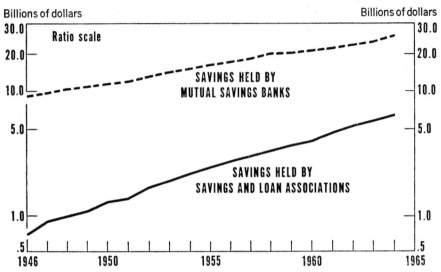

Spreads Between the Average Annual Net Growth Rates of Savings and Loan Associations and Mutual Savings Banks in New York, 1946–1964

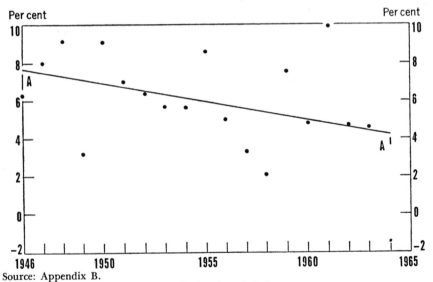

Source: Appendix B.

Note: The equation for line AA' and related statistical measurements are:

$$SLA_{growth\,rate} - MSB_{growth\,rate} = 7.76 - .19x \qquad R^2 = .17$$
$$(.06)$$

APPENDIX CHART 4

Spreads Between the Average Annual Net Growth Rates
of Savings and Loan Associations and Mutual
Savings Banks in New York City and in
New York Excluding New York City,
1953–1964

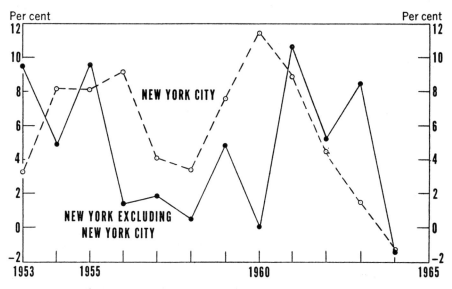

Source: Appendix B.

APPENDIX CHART 5

Spreads Between the Average Annual Net Growth Rates of Savings and Loan Associations and Mutual Savings Banks in Massachusetts and Connecticut, 1946–1964

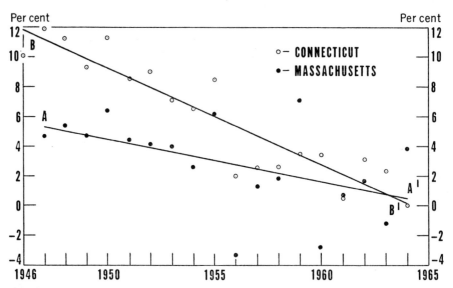

Source: Appendix B.

Note: In Massachusetts, the 1946 spread of 19.2 per cent is not typical of post-1945 behavior and is therefore omitted from the computations. The equation for line AA′ and related statistical measures are:

$$SLA_{growth\,rate} - MSB_{growth\,rate} = 5.61 - .28x \qquad R^2 = .31$$
$$(.09)$$

The equation for line BB′—drawn through the observations for Connecticut—and accompanying statistical indicators are:

$$SLA_{growth\,rate} - MSB_{growth\,rate} = 12.46 - .67x \qquad R^2 = .85$$
$$(.06)$$

APPENDIX CHART 6
Gross Savings in Mutual Savings Banks and Savings and Loan
Associations in Pennsylvania, New Jersey,
and Maryland, 1945–1964

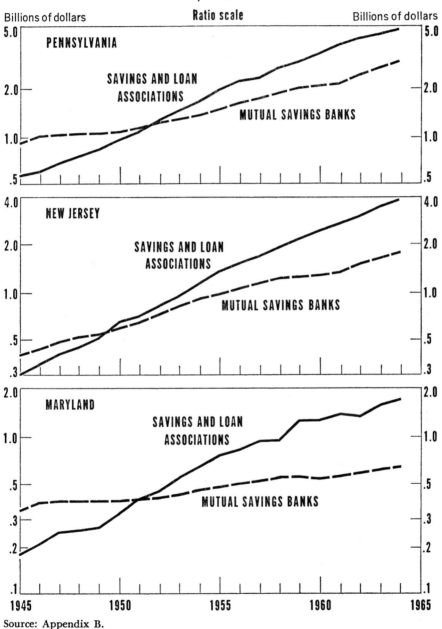

Source: Appendix B.

APPENDIX CHART 7
Gross Savings in Mutual Savings Banks and Savings and
Loan Associations in the Twelve Smallest
Mutual Savings Bank States, 1945–1964

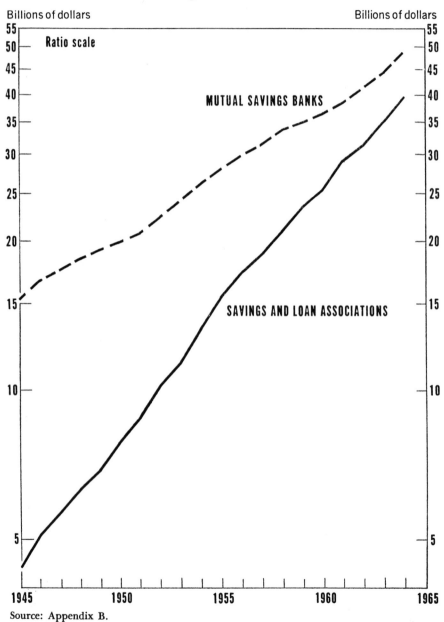

Source: Appendix B.

Spreads Between the Average Annual Net Growth Rates
of Savings and Loan Associations and Mutual
Savings Banks in the Twelve Smallest
Mutual Savings Bank States,
1946–1964

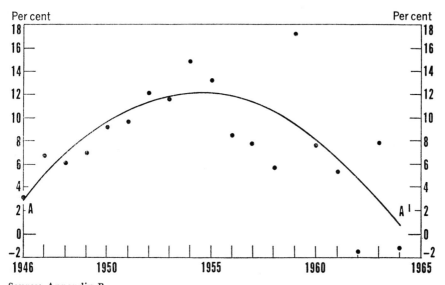

Source: Appendix B.
Note: The equation for line AA' and related statistical measures are:
$$SLA_{growth\ rate} - MSB_{growth\ rate} = 2.56 + 2.38x - .14x^2 \qquad R^2 = .61$$
$$(.55) \quad (.02)$$

APPENDIX CHART 9
Number of Savings Accounts in Mutual Savings Banks and
in Savings and Loan Associations in New York, 1949–1964

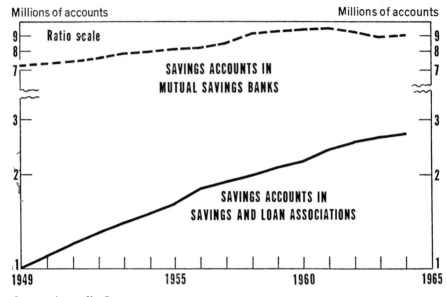

Source: Appendix C.

Appendix B: Savings in Mutual Savings Banks and Savings and Loan Associations, Selected Regions, 1945–1964

APPENDIX TABLE 1

Savings in Mutual Savings Banks and Savings and Loan Associations,
Selected Regions, 1945–1964
(*In billions of dollars*)

Year	All SLA			SLA in MSB States			All MSB		
	Gross	Net[a]	Per-centage Change[b]	Gross	Net	Per-centage Change	Gross	Net	Per-centage Change
1945	7.386	7.228		4.361	4.266		15.331	15.094	
1946	8.548	8.368	13.3	5.085	4.981	14.2	16.813	16.587	8.2
1947	9.750	9.558	11.8	5.714	5.598	10.1	17.759	17.473	3.9
1948	10.964	10.740	10.2	6.280	6.149	7.6	18.400	18.081	1.8
1949	12.472	12.221	11.5	6.879	6.735	7.2	19.287	18.646	1.3
1950	13.978	13.661	9.5	7.816	7.644	11.1	20.025	19.659	1.9
1951	16.073	15.710	12.4	8.820	8.617	10.2	20.900	20.500	2.4
1952	19.148	18.714	16.4	10.160	9.922	12.5	22.610	22.109	5.8
1953	22.778	22.242	16.2	11.350	11.066	8.9	24.388	23.823	5.4
1954	27.164	26.504	16.4	13.401	13.072	15.2	26.351	25.717	5.4
1955	32.058	31.270	15.1	15.645	15.191	13.4	28.182	27.471	4.3
1956	37.073	36.111	12.6	17.311	16.792	7.3	30.026	29.185	3.6
1957	41.856	40.633	9.6	18.978	18.407	6.3	31.684	30.784	2.5
1958	47.894	46.513	11.1	21.138	20.512	8.1	34.031	33.049	4.3
1959	54.583	52.907	10.5	23.655	22.827	8.0	34.977	33.888	− .4
1960	62.142	60.013	9.9	25.690	25.037	5.8	36.343	35.084	.3
1961	70.838	68.290	9.9	29.220	28.297	10.1	38.277	37.018	1.9
1962	80.400	76.943	8.6	31.576	30.360	3.9	41.336	39.805	4.0
1963	91.205	87.557	8.9	35.397	33.981	7.6	44.606	42.822	3.6
1964	101.847	97.508	6.9	39.454	37.797	6.8	48.849	46.845	5.0

Sources: United States Savings and Loan League, *Savings and Loan Annals;* National Association of Mutual Savings Banks, *Annual Report: Facts and Figures;* Savings Banks Association of New York; New York Savings and Loan League.

[a] "Net" = gross – annual interest payments.
[b] "Percentage change = net savings ÷ gross savings of previous year.

APPENDIX TABLE 1 (*continued*)

	SLA in New York State				*MSB in New York State*		
Year	*Gross*	*Net*	*Percentage Change*		*Gross*	*Net*	*Percentage Change*
1945	.634	.618			8.292	8.151	
1946	.747	.729	15.0		9.170	9.014	8.7
1947	.866	.846	13.3		9.814	9.647	5.2
1948	.999	.976	12.7		10.340	10.153	3.5
1949	1.108	1.083	8.4		11.102	10.891	5.3
1950	1.275	1.243	12.2		11.662	11.429	2.9
1951	1.430	1.393	9.3		12.188	11.932	2.3
1952	1.658	1.613	12.8		13.276	12.957	6.3
1953	1.896	1.843	11.2		14.360	14.001	5.5
1954	2.161	2.098	10.7		15.492	15.089	5.1
1955	2.505	2.432	12.5		16.544	16.110	4.0
1956	2.809	2.734	9.1		17.657	17.162	3.7
1957	3.075	2.973	5.8		18.649	18.089	2.4
1958	3.392	3.280	6.7		20.112	19.489	4.5
1959	3.781	3.649	7.6		20.715	20.052	− .3
1960	4.124	3.963	4.8		21.436	20.664	− .2
1961	4.751	4.556	10.5		22.406	21.577	.7
1962	5.340	5.110	7.6		23.997	23.037	2.8
1963	5.983	5.956	7.7		25.772	24.741	3.1
1964	6.443	6.189	3.4		28.339	27.117	5.2

	SLA in New York City				*MSB in New York City*		
1952	.823	.800			10.6	10.3	
1953	.923	.897	9.0		11.5	11.2	5.7
1954	1.069	1.038	12.5		12.4	12.0	4.3
1955	1.236	1.200	12.3		13.2	12.9	4.0
1956	1.440	1.397	13.0		14.1	13.7	3.8
1957	1.593	1.540	6.9		14.9	14.5	2.8
1958	1.780	1.721	8.0		16.1	15.6	4.7
1959	1.987	1.917	7.7		16.5	15.9	−1.2
1960	2.286	2.197	10.6		17.0	16.5	.0
1961	2.598	2.491	9.0		17.7	17.0	.0
1962	2.898	2.773	6.7		18.9	18.1	2.3
1963	3.193	3.046	5.1		20.4	19.6	3.7
1964	3.447	3.302	3.4		22.4	21.5	5.4

	SLA in New York State Outside of New York City				*MSB in New York State Outside of New York City*		
1952	.835	.812			2.7	2.6	
1953	.973	.946	13.3		2.9	2.8	3.7
1954	1.092	1.060	8.9		3.1	3.0	3.4
1955	1.269	1.232	12.8		3.3	3.2	3.2
1956	1.369	1.328	4.6		3.6	3.5	6.0
1957	1.482	1.433	4.7		3.8	3.7	2.8
1958	1.612	1.559	5.2		4.0	3.9	2.6
1959	1.794	1.731	7.4		4.2	4.1	2.5
1960	1.838	1.766	−1.6		4.4	4.2	.0

APPENDIX TABLE 1 (*continued*)

Year	Gross	Net	Percentage Change	Gross	Net	Percentage Change
1961	2.153	2.065	12.3	4.7	4.5	2.3
1962	2.442	2.336	8.5	5.1	4.9	4.3
1963	2.801	2.698	10.5	5.4	5.2	2.0
1964	3.049	2.921	4.3	6.0	5.7	5.6

	SLA in Massachusetts			*MSB in Massachusetts*		
1945	.472	.460		2.856	2.807	
1946	.605	.590	25.1	3.081	3.029	6.1
1947	.655	.640	5.8	3.167	3.113	1.0
1948	.704	.688	5.0	3.210	3.152	– .5
1949	.754	.737	4.7	3.249	3.187	– .7
1950	.823	.802	6.4	3.312	3.245	– .1
1951	.890	.867	5.3	3.413	3.341	.9
1952	.984	.957	7.5	3.615	3.528	3.4
1953	1.094	1.063	8.0	3.861	3.764	4.1
1954	1.213	1.178	7.7	4.162	4.054	5.0
1955	1.386	1.346	11.0	4.484	4.363	4.8
1956	1.428	1.385	– .1	4.767	4.634	3.3
1957	1.513	1.462	2.4	4.973	4.824	1.2
1958	1.639	1.585	4.8	5.286	5.122	3.0
1959	1.819	1.775	8.3	5.519	5.342	1.1
1960	1.854	1.782	–2.0	5.793	5.584	1.2
1961	2.007	1.927	3.9	6.204	5.974	3.1
1962	2.204	2.110	5.1	6.689	6.421	3.5
1963	2.358	2.259	2.5	7.223	6.934	3.7
1964	2.658	2.546	8.0	7.867	7.544	4.4

	SLA in Connecticut			*MSB in Connecticut*		
1945	.093	.091		1.115	1.096	
1946	.112	.109	17.2	1.215	1.194	7.1
1947	.132	.129	15.2	1.276	1.254	3.2
1948	.150	.147	11.4	1.300	1.276	.0
1949	.168	.164	9.3	1.321	1.296	– .3
1950	.192	.187	11.3	1.335	1.308	–1.0
1951	.218	.212	10.4	1.390	1.360	1.9
1952	.254	.247	13.3	1.487	1.451	4.4
1953	.291	.283	11.4	1.602	1.561	5.0
1954	.333	.323	11.0	1.720	1.675	4.6
1955	.386	.375	12.6	1.841	1.791	4.1
1956	.425	.412	6.7	1.985	1.929	4.8
1957	.462	.447	5.2	2.102	2.038	2.7
1958	.509	.492	6.5	2.256	2.186	4.0
1959	.559	.539	5.9	2.386	2.310	2.4
1960	.611	.587	5.0	2.516	2.425	1.6
1961	.664	.637	4.3	2.712	2.611	3.8
1962	.746	.714	7.5	2.952	2.834	4.5
1963	.820	.788	5.6	3.197	3.069	4.0
1964	.885	.848	3.4	3.452	3.307	3.4

APPENDIX TABLE 1 (*continued*)

	SLA in Pennsylvania			MSB in Pennsylvania		
Year	Gross	Net	Percentage Change	Gross	Net	Percentage Change
1945	.574	.559		.932	.916	
1946	.600	.585	1.9	1.007	.990	6.2
1947	.679	.663	10.5	1.039	1.021	1.4
1948	.752	.734	8.1	1.050	1.031	− .8
1949	.830	.810	7.7	1.062	1.042	− .8
1950	.964	.940	13.3	1.076	1.055	− .7
1951	1.081	1.053	9.2	1.136	1.112	3.3
1952	1.242	1.208	11.7	1.222	1.193	5.0
1953	1.447	1.406	13.2	1.297	1.264	3.4
1954	1.677	1.628	12.5	1.380	1.344	3.6
1955	1.964	1.909	13.8	1.497	1.456	5.5
1956	2.228	2.161	10.0	1.612	1.567	4.7
1957	2.369	2.291	2.8	1.734	1.682	4.3
1958	2.717	2.627	10.9	1.892	1.833	5.7
1959	2.984	2.880	6.0	2.000	1.936	2.3
1960	3.366	3.235	8.4	2.090	2.014	.7
1961	3.833	3.676	9.2	2.180	2.099	.4
1962	4.144	3.965	3.4	2.435	2.337	7.2
1963	4.423	4.246	2.5	2.697	2.589	6.3
1964	4.742	4.551	2.9	2.966	2.841	5.3

	SLA in New Jersey			MSB in New Jersey		
1945	.301	.293		.408	.401	
1946	.354	.346	15.0	.448	.440	7.8
1947	.409	.399	12.7	.505	.496	10.7
1948	.450	.440	7.6	.526	.516	2.2
1949	.510	.498	10.7	.546	.536	1.9
1950	.600	.585	14.7	.599	.587	7.5
1951	.705	.687	14.5	.663	.649	8.3
1952	.823	.801	13.6	.753	.735	10.9
1953	.948	.921	11.9	.838	.817	8.5
1954	1.140	1.107	16.8	.938	.913	8.9
1955	1.372	1.332	16.8	1.010	.983	4.8
1956	1.531	1.485	8.2	1.099	1.068	5.7
1957	1.703	1.647	7.6	1.180	1.144	4.1
1958	1.935	1.871	9.9	1.278	1.238	4.9
1959	2.183	2.107	8.9	1.315	1.273	− .4
1960	2.426	2.331	6.8	1.347	1.298	−1.3
1961	2.736	2.623	8.1	1.410	1.359	.9
1962	3.048	2.917	6.6	1.575	1.512	7.2
1963	3.484	3.358	10.2	1.723	1.654	5.0
1964	3.800	3.640	4.5	1.864	1.790	3.9

	SLA in Maryland			MSB in Maryland		
1945	.184	.179		.349	.343	
1946	.219	.214	16.3	.383	.376	7.7
1947	.252	.246	12.3	.394	.387	1.0
1948	.267	.261	3.6	.395	.388	−1.5

APPENDIX TABLE 1 (*continued*)

Year	Gross	Net	Percentage Change	Gross	Net	Percentage Change
1949	.275	.269	.7	.398	.390	−1.3
1950	.314	.332	20.7	.402	.394	−1.0
1951	.417	.406	29.3	.407	.398	−1.0
1952	.469	.456	9.4	.422	.412	1.2
1953	.576	.560	19.4	.444	.433	2.6
1954	.667	.647	12.3	.469	.457	2.9
1955	.783	.760	13.9	.490	.477	1.7
1956	.865	.839	7.2	.511	.497	1.4
1957	.970	.938	8.4	.539	.523	2.3
1958	.979	.947	−2.4	.567	.549	1.9
1959	1.272	1.227	25.3	.570	.552	−2.6
1960	1.314	1.262	− .8	.561	.541	−5.1
1961	1.428	1.387	5.6	.579	.555	−1.1
1962	1.373	1.319	−7.6	.606	.582	.5
1963	1.642	1.576	14.8	.633	.608	.3
1964	1.773	1.698	3.4	.670	.642	1.4

	SLA in 12 Smallest MSB States			MSB in 12 Smallest MSB States		
1945	2.163	2.108		1.380	1.356	
1946	2.448	2.389	10.4	1.509	1.482	7.4
1947	2.721	2.658	8.6	1.564	1.536	1.8
1948	2.958	2.890	6.2	1.579	1.550	− .9
1949	3.234	3.159	7.0	1.613	1.578	− .1
1950	3.621	3.531	9.2	1.639	1.583	−1.9
1951	4.079	3.974	9.7	1.703	1.623	−1.0
1952	4.701	4.575	12.2	1.835	1.705	.1
1953	5.398	5.246	11.6	1.986	1.835	.0
1954	6.220	6.204	14.9	2.190	1.996	.5
1955	7.260	7.040	13.2	2.316	2.189	.0
1956	8.117	7.868	8.4	2.395	2.303	− .6
1957	8.981	8.721	7.4	2.507	2.391	− .2
1958	9.975	9.675	7.7	2.640	2.557	2.0
1959	11.151	10.754	7.8	2.472	2.392	− 9.4
1960	12.265	11.787	5.7	2.620	2.426	− 1.9
1961	13.777	13.212	7.7	2.786	2.682	2.4
1962	15.078	14.430	4.7	3.082	2.958	6.2
1963	17.691	16.983	12.6	3.361	3.227	4.7
1964	19.203	18.396	4.0	3.686	3.535	5.2

	SLA in California		
Year	Gross	Net	Percentage Change
1945	.557	.545	
1946	.648	.634	13.8
1947	.784	.766	18.2
1948	.842	.823	5.0
1949	.999	.976	15.9
1950	1.166	1.139	14.0
1951	1.394	1.360	16.6

APPENDIX TABLE 1 *(continued)*

SLA in California

Year	Gross	Net	Percentage Change
1952	1.749	1.703	22.2
1953	2.227	2.166	23.8
1954	2.776	2.698	21.1
1955	3.413	3.327	19.8
1956	4.259	4.118	20.7
1957	4.987	4.812	13.0
1958	6.101	5.875	17.8
1959	7.338	7.059	15.7
1960	8.889	8.524	16.2
1961	10.849	10.382	16.8
1962	13.353	12.752	17.5
1963	16.353	15.699	17.6
1964	19.300	18.489	13.1

Appendix C: Number of Savings Accounts in Mutual Savings Banks and Savings and Loan Associations, Selected Regions, 1949–1964

APPENDIX TABLE 2

Number of Savings Accounts in Mutual Savings Banks and Savings and
Loan Associations, Selected Regions, 1949–1964

(*In thousands*)

| | SLA Accounts | | | | | | MSB Accounts | | | |
Year	Total	Per-centage Change	In MSB States	Per-centage Change	In New York	Per-centage Change	Total	Per-centage Change	In New York	Per-centage Change
1949	9.885		5.540		.980		19.182		7.309	
1950	10.674	8.0	6.123	10.5	1.083	10.5	19.264	0.4	7.441	1.8
1951	11.810	10.6	6.518	6.5	1.157	6.8	19.406	0.7	7.515	1.0
1952	13.120	11.1	7.091	8.8	1.275	10.2	19.881	2.4	7.722	2.8
1953	14.748	12.4	7.706	8.7	1.419	11.3	20.218	1.7	7.861	1.8
1954	16.432	11.4	8.525	10.6	1.523	7.3	20.565	1.7	8.010	1.9
1955	18.107	10.2	9.271	8.8	1.614	6.0	21.001	2.1	8.198	2.3
1956	20.508	13.3	9.894	6.7	1.763	9.2	21.382	1.8	8.317	1.5
1957	22.285	8.7	10.982	11.0	1.882	6.7	21.713	1.5	8.528	2.5
1958	24.353	9.3	11.554	5.2	1.970	4.7	22.281	2.6	9.056	6.2
1959	26.653	9.4	12.350	6.9	2.078	5.5	22.291	0	9.251	2.2
1960	29.453	10.5	13.149	6.5	2.217	6.7	22.493	0.9	9.442	2.1
1961	33.428	13.5	14.031	6.7	2.400	8.3	22.553	0.3	9.498	0.6
1962	34.902	4.4	15.242	8.6	2.562	6.8	22.490	−0.3	9.316	−1.9
1963	36.913	5.8	16.021	5.1	2.640	3.0	22.003	−2.2	8.894	−4.5
1964	38.900	5.4	16.533	3.2	2.685	1.7	22.231	1.0	8.987	1.0

Sources: United States Savings and Loan League, *Savings and Loan Annals;*
National Association of Mutual Savings Banks, *Annual Report: Facts and Fig-
ures;* Savings Banks Association of New York; Savings Association League of New
York.

Appendix D: Location of Mutual Savings Banks and Savings and Loan Associations in New York City

DIFFERENCES IN TOTAL personal income are found not only between urban and nonurban regions but also between smaller areas such as city boroughs or even city blocks. Thus, if differences in location provide an underlying explanation for the persistent spread between the growth rates of savings and loan associations and mutual savings banks, one would expect the data for New York City to verify this as clearly as do the figures for all of New York State. Tables 3 and 4 in this appendix indicate that this is precisely the case.

Table 3 records for 1963 the number of main and branch offices of mutual savings banks and savings and loan associations in New York City, both inside and outside the borough containing the home office. The data indicate that there were 18 mutual savings banks in Manhattan and that all but one of their 53 branches were in the same borough. The 18 savings and loan associations in Manhattan, on the other hand, had 26 branches, and all but 7 of these were in *other* boroughs. Moreover, the mutual savings bank offices in Manhattan comprised 36 per cent of all mutual savings bank offices and 59 per cent of all mutual savings bank deposits in New York City. The savings and loan association offices in Manhattan, on the other hand, comprised only 16 per cent of the offices and only 29 per cent of the savings in all New York City savings and loan associations.

With mutual savings banks more highly concentrated than savings and loan associations in Manhattan, it is important to see if there were any significant differences in changes in total personal income between Manhattan and the other four boroughs. Table 4 shows that there were. Of New York City's five boroughs, Manhattan had the sharpest decline in population, the lowest median income (for families and unrelated individuals), and the smallest increase in total family income from 1949 through 1959.[1]

---

[1] In addition, most of the mutual savings banks in Manhattan were organized earlier than most of the savings and loan associations. Thus most mutual savings bank offices are in the borough's oldest sections, neighborhoods that currently contain the lowest income levels and that have recently experienced the largest population declines.

APPENDIX TABLE 3

Location of Main and Branch Offices of Mutual Savings Banks and
Savings and Loan Associations in New York, August 31, 1963

	Number of Principal Offices	Number of Branch Offices		Total Offices
		In the Home Community [a]	*Outside the Home Community*	
New York State				
MSB	126	159	36	321
SLA	227	71	75	373
Manhattan				
MSB	18	52	1	71
SLA	18	7	19	44
Bronx				
MSB	3	11	0	14
SLA	3	2	0	5
Brooklyn				
MSB	21	42	12	75
SLA	11	4	4	19
Queens				
MSB	7	19	2	28
SLA	19	23	5	47
Richmond				
MSB	2	5	0	7
SLA	10	8	0	18

Source: Savings Banks Association of New York State, "Locations of Main
Offices and Branches of Commercial Banks, Savings Banks, and Savings and Loan
Associations in New York State, 1963" (New York: Savings Banks Association of
New York State, 1963), selected pages.
[a] The "home community" is the borough containing the main office.

APPENDIX TABLE 4

Population, Median Income and Changes in Total Family Income
in the Boroughs of New York City, 1949 and 1959

	Population (in thousands)				
Year	*Manhattan*	*Bronx*	*Brooklyn*	*Queens*	*Richmond*
1949	1,960	1,451	2,738	1,550	191
1959	1,698	1,424	2,627	1,809	222
1949–59	− 13.4%	− 1.9%	− 4.1%	+ 16.7%	+ 16.2%
Median Income for Families and Unrelated Individuals					
1949	$2,347	$3,297	$3,151	$3,817	$3,443
1959	3,923	5,106	5,106	6,443	6,173
1949–59	+ 67.1%	+ 62.0%	+ 62.0%	+ 68.7%	+ 70.3%
Changes in Total Family Income					
1949–59	+ 145%	+ 152%	+ 150%	+ 219%	+ 207%

Source: U.S. Bureau of the Census, Department of Commerce, *U.S. Census of
Population and Housing, 1960, Final Report*, Vol. 104, Pt. 1 (Washington, D.C.:
Government Printing Office, 1962).

In Brooklyn, the borough with the next lowest increase in total family income, mutual savings banks had 32 per cent of their New York City offices, compared to only 11 per cent for savings and loan associations.[2] In the Bronx, with a 1.9 per cent population decline and a 62 per cent gain in median family income, there were 14 mutual savings bank offices and only 5 savings and loan associations.

But in Queens and Richmond, the only boroughs with increasing populations and the two with the most rapidly growing median family incomes, savings and loan associations had 49 per cent of their New York City offices compared to only 17 per cent for mutual savings banks.

Thus, mutual savings banks in New York City were in boroughs experiencing the smallest gains in total personal income to a significantly greater extent than were savings and loan associations. This is clearly consistent with previous findings indicating that differences in location provide a fundamental explanation for the spread between the average growth rates of the two industries during the post-1945 period.

[2] The twelve mutual savings bank offices outside the home community were established pursuant to the Omnibus Banking Act of 1960.

Selected Bibliography

PRINTED MATERIAL

Alberts, William W. "Business Cycles, Residential Construction Cycles, and the Mortgage Market," *Journal of Political Economy,* Vol. LXX (June, 1962).

Alhadeff, David. "A Reconsideration of Restrictions on Bank Entry," *Quarterly Journal of Economics,* Vol. LXXVI (May, 1962).

Alhadeff, David, and Charlotte Alhadeff. "The Struggle for Commercial Bank Savings," *Quarterly Journal of Economics,* Vol. LXXII (February, 1958).

American Bankers Association. *The Commercial Banking Industry.* Englewood Cliffs, N.J.: Prentice-Hall, 1962.

American Bankers Association, Savings Division. *Response to Change: A Century of Commercial Bank Activity in the Savings Field.* New York: American Bankers Association, 1965.

Aschheim, Joseph. "Commercial Banks and Financial Intermediaries: Fallacies and Policy Implications," *Journal of Political Economy,* Vol. LXVII (February, 1959).

Baxter, Nevins D., David McFarland, and Harold T. Shapiro. "Banking Structure and Nonbank Financial Intermediaries," *National Banking Review,* Vol. IV (March, 1967).

Bellman, Harold. *The Building Society Movement.* London: Methuen and Co., Ltd., 1927.

Berle, Adolf A. *The Bank That Banks Built.* New York: Harper & Brothers, 1959.

Board of Governors of the Federal Reserve System. *Federal Reserve Bulletin.* Washington, D.C.: Board of Governors of the Federal Reserve System, 1946–64.

Bodfish, Morton, ed. *History of the Building and Loan in the United States.* Chicago: United States Building and Loan League, 1931.

Bodfish, Morton, and A. D. Theobald. *Savings and Loan Principles.* Englewood Cliffs, N.J.: Prentice-Hall, 1940.

Bogen, Jules I. "Trends in the Institutionalization of Savings and in Thrift Institution Policies," *Conference on Savings and Residential Financing, 1960 Proceedings.* Chicago: United States Savings and Loan League, 1960.

Bogen, Jules I., ed. *Economic Study of Savings Banking in New York State.* New York: Savings Banks Association of New York, 1956.

Brabook, Henry W. "Statistics of Building Societies," *Yearbook of the United States Building and Loan League, 1930.* Chicago: United States Building and Loan League, 1931.

"Branch Laws for Savings Banks Strike Multiple of Dissonant Chords," *Savings Bank Journal,* Vol. XLVIII (February, 1963).

Brill, Daniel H., and Ann P. Ulrey. "The Role of Financial Intermediaries in the U.S. Capital Markets," Board of Governors of the Federal Reserve System, *Federal Reserve Bulletin,* January, 1967.

Cacy, J. A. "Financial Intermediaries and the Postwar Home Mortgage Market," Federal Reserve Bank of Kansas City, *Monthly Review,* January-February, 1967.

Chamberlin, Edward. *The Theory of Monopolistic Competition.* Cambridge, Mass.: Harvard University Press, 1934.

Chandler, Lester V. "Monopolistic Elements in Commercial Bankings," *Journal of Political Economy,* Vol. XLVI (February, 1938).

Clark, Horace F., and Frank A. Chase. *Elements of the Modern Building and Loan Association.* New York: The Macmillan Company, 1925.

Commission on Money and Credit. *Money and Credit: Their Influence on Jobs, Prices, and Growth.* Englewood Cliffs, N.J.: Prentice-Hall, 1961.

Conway, Lawrence V. *Savings and Loan Principles.* Chicago: American Savings and Loan Institute Press, 1957.

Cox, [Reverend]. *Mutual Benefit Building and Loan Associations: Their History, Principles, and Plan of Operations.* Charleston: Brown and Co., 1852.

Davis, Richard, and Lois Banks. "Interregional Interest Rate Differentials," in Federal Reserve Bank of New York, *Monthly Review,* August, 1965.

Dexter, Seymour. *Cooperative Savings and Loan Associations.* New York: Appleton-Century, 1889.

Entine, Alan D. "Government Securities Holdings of Selected Financial Intermediaries, 1954–1962," *Journal of Finance,* Vol. XIX (December, 1964).

Ettin, Edward C. "The Development of American Financial Intermediaries," *Quarterly Review of Economics and Business,* Vol. III (Summer, 1963).

Ewalt, Josephine. *A Business Reborn.* Chicago: United States Savings and Loan League, 1961.

Federal Deposit Insurance Corporation, *Annual Report.* Washington, D.C.: Federal Deposit Insurance Corporation, 1946–64.

Federal Home Loan Bank Board. *Combined Financial Statements.* Washington, D.C.: Federal Home Loan Bank Board, 1947–64.

Federal Home Loan Bank System. *Federal Home Loan Bank Review.* Washington, D.C.: Federal Home Loan Bank System, October, 1934.

—— *Twentieth Anniversary Booklet, 1952.* Washington, D.C.: Federal Home Loan Bank System, 1952.

Federal Reserve Bank of Boston. "Interest Rates Paid on Savings," *New England Business Review,* March, 1962.

Federal Reserve Bank of New York. "Time and Savings Deposits at Member Banks," *Monthly Review,* July, 1960.

Feige, Edgar L. *The Demand for Liquid Assets: A Temporal Cross-Section Analysis.* Englewood Cliffs, N.J.: Prentice-Hall, 1963.

Foundation for Commercial Banks. *The Politz Study of Consumer Attitudes toward Commercial Banks.* Philadelphia: Foundation for Commercial Banks, 1963.

Freeman, Gaylord A., Jr. *Mutual Competition.* Chicago: The First National Bank of Chicago, 1958.

—— "Savings and Loan Competition as Seen by a Banker," *Savings and Loan Journal,* February, 1956.

Freund, William C. "Financial Intermediaries and Federal Reserve Controls over the Business Cycle," *Quarterly Review of Economics and Business,* Vol. II (February, 1962).

Friend, Irwin. "Determinants of the Volume and Composition of Savings," in Commission on Money and Credit, *Impacts of Monetary Policy.* Englewood Cliffs, N.J.: Prentice-Hall, 1963.

—— "The Effects of Monetary Policies on Nonmonetary Financial Institutions and Capital Markets," in Commission on Money and Credit, *Private Capital Markets.* Englewood Cliffs, N.J.: Prentice-Hall, 1964.

Geis, Thomas G., Thomas Mayer, and Edward C. Ettin. "Portfolio Regulations and Policies of Financial Intermediaries," in Commission on Money and Credit, *Private Financial Institutions.* Englewood Cliffs, N.J.: Prentice-Hall, 1963.

Goldsmith, Raymond W. *Financial Intermediaries in the American Economy since 1900.* Princeton, N.J.: Princeton University Press, 1958.

—— *A Study of Saving in the United States.* Vol. I. Princeton, N.J.: Princeton University Press, 1955.

Grebler, Leo, David M. Blank, and Louis Winnick. *Capital Formation in Residential Real Estate.* Princeton, N.J.: Princeton University Press, 1956.

Grebler, Leo, and Eugene F. Brigham. *Savings and Mortgage Markets in California.* Pasadena, Calif.: California Savings and Loan League, 1963.

Gurley, John G. "Financial Institutions in the Saving-Investment Process," *Conference on Savings and Residential Financing, 1959 Proceedings.* Chicago: United States Savings and Loan League, 1959.

—— "Liquidity and Financial Institutions in the Postwar Economy," in *Employment, Growth and Price Level: Study Paper #14,* Prepared for the Joint Economic Committee. 86th Congress, 2d session, January 25, 1960.

Gurley, John G., and Edward S. Shaw. "Financial Aspects of Economic Development," *American Economic Review,* Vol. XLV (September, 1955).

—— "Financial Intermediaries and the Savings-Investment Process," *Journal of Finance,* Vol. XI (May, 1956).

—— *Money in a Theory of Finance.* Washington, D.C.: Brookings Institute, 1960.

Harriss, C. Lowell. *History and Policies of the Home Owners' Loan Corporation.* New York: National Bureau of Economic Research, 1951.

Hicks, J. R. "A Suggestion for Simplifying the Theory of Money," in *Readings in Monetary Theory.* Homewood, Ill.: Richard D. Irwin, 1951. Reprinted from *Economica,* New Series, 2, 1935.

Horne, Oliver H. *A History of Savings Banks.* London: Oxford University Press, 1947.

Ihlefeld, August. "Savings Bank Liquidity," *United States Investor,* May 2, 1960.

Jones, Gordon H., and Charles E. Rauch. "Liquidity—What Is Adequate?" *Savings Bank Journal,* August, 1959.

Keith, Gordon E. "The Impact of Federal Taxation on the Flow of Personal Savings Through Investment Intermediaries," in Commission on Money and Credit, *Private Financial Institutions.* Englewood Cliffs, N.J.: Prentice-Hall, 1963.

Kendall, Leon T. "The New Environment Facing Financial Intermediaries in the Next Decade," *Conference on Savings and Residential Financing, 1963.* Chicago: United States Savings and Loan League, 1963.

—— *The Savings and Loan Business.* Englewood Cliffs, N.J.: Prentice-Hall, 1962.

—— "Savings in the American Economy," *Conference on Savings and Residential Financing, 1961 Proceedings.* Chicago: United States Savings and Loan League, 1961.

Keyes, Emerson W. *A History of Savings Banking in the United States, 1816–1877.* Vols. I, II. New York: Bradford Rhodes, 1878.

—— *A History of Savings Banks in the State of New York.* Albany, N.Y.: Argus Company Printers, 1870.

Keynes, John M. *The General Theory of Employment, Interest and Money.* New York: Harcourt, Brace, and World, 1936.

Klaman, Saul B. "NAMSB Survey of Out-of-State Mortgage Lending by Savings Banks," *Savings Bank Journal,* April, 1963.

—— *The Postwar Residential Mortgage Market,* Princeton, N.J.: Princeton University Press, 1961.

—— *The Volume of Mortgage Debt in the Postwar Decade.* New York: National Bureau of Economic Research, Inc., 1958.

Klaman, Saul B., and Donald Lawson. "For Savings Banks and S & L's—The Choice Is Change . . . Or Else," *Challenge,* Vol. XV (July-August, 1967).

Knowles, Charles E. *History of The Bank for Savings in the City of New York, 1819–1929.* New York: The Bank for Savings in the City of New York, 1929.

Kreps, Clifton H., Jr., and David T. Lapkin. *Improving the Competition for Funds Between Commercial Banks and Thrift Institutions.* Chapel Hill, N.C.: School of Business Administration, University of North Carolina, 1963.

—— "Public Regulation and Operating Conventions Affecting Sources of Funds of Commercial Banks and Thrift Institutions," *Journal of Finance,* Vol. XVII (May, 1962).

Langford, John A. *A Century of Birmingham Life; or, A Chronicle of Local Events, 1741–1841.* Birmingham: E. C. Osborne, 1868.

Leaver, J. B. "The Historical and Legal Development of British Building Societies," *Yearbook of the United States Building and Loan League, 1894.* Chicago: United States Building and Loan League, 1895.

Lee, Tong Hun. "Substitutability of Non-Bank Intermediary Liabilities for Money: The Empirical Evidence," *Journal of Finance,* Vol. XXI (September, 1966).

Lerner, Eugene M. "An Analysis of Home Office Protection," State of New York, *Legislative Document No. 14,* March 15, 1963.

Lewins, William. *A History of Banks for Savings.* London: Sampson, Low, Son, and Marston, 1886.

Lintner, John. *Mutual Savings Banks in the Savings and Mortgage Markets.* Boston: Harvard University, Graduate School of Business Administration, 1948.

Mayer, Thomas. "Is Portfolio Control of Financial Institutions Justified?" *Journal of Finance,* Vol. XVII (May, 1962).

Motter, David C., and Deane Carson. "Bank Entry and the Public Interest: A Case Study," *National Banking Review,* Vol. I, No. 4 (June, 1964).

Myers, Holtby R. "The California Guarantee Stock Plan," *American Building Association News,* Vol. XLI (December, 1921).

Nadler, Marcus, and associates. *The Banking Situation in New York State.* New York: New York State Bankers Association, 1956.

Nadler, Paul S. *The Future of Savings Banking in New York State.* New York: New York University Graduate School of Business, 1961.

National Association of Mutual Savings Banks. *Annual Report.* New York: National Association of Mutual Savings Banks, 1960–65.

—— *Directory and Guide.* New York: National Association of Mutual Savings Banks, 1965–66.

—— *Mutual Savings Banking: Basic Characteristics and Role in the National Economy.* Englewood Cliffs, N.J.: Prentice-Hall, 1962.

New York State Bankers Association. *Banks and the Future of New York State.* New York: New York State Bankers Association, 1964.

Prather, William. "The Modern Savings Account Concept," United States Savings and Loan League, *Legal Bulletin,* Vol. XXIII, No. 47 (May, 1957).

Prochnow, Herbert V., ed. *American Financial Institutions.* New York: Harper & Brothers, 1951.

Rosenthal, Henry S. *Cyclopedia of Building and Loan Associations.* Cincinnati: American Building Association News, 1939.

Rosenthal, Henry S., and Robert B. Jacoby. *Cyclopedia of Federal Savings and Loan Associations.* Cincinnati: American Building Association News, 1939.

Rozen, Marvin E. "The Changing Structure of Financial Institutions," *Quarterly Review of Economics and Business,* Vol. II (November, 1962).

—— "Competition among Financial Institutions for Demand and Thrift Deposits," *Journal of Finance,* Vol. XVII (May, 1962).

Russell, Horace, and William Prather. "Legal Aspects of Savings Accounts," United States Savings and Loan League, *Legal Bulletin,* Vol. XXV, No. 1 (September, 1959).

Sanborn, Frank B. "Cooperative Building Associations," *Publication of the American Social Science Associations,* September 7, 1888.

Savings Banks Association of New York State. "The Savings Banks of New York State: Their Need to Grow and Expand in the Interests of the People and the Economy of the State." New York: Savings Banks Association of New York State, 1964.

—— "Study of Bank Office Locations Reveals 'Imbalance,' " *Savings Bank Depositor,* Vol. VII (January–February, 1965).

Schweiger, Irving, and John S. McGee. *Chicago Banking.* Chicago: University of Chicago, Graduate School of Business, 1961.

Scratchley, Arthur. *A Practical Treatise on Savings Banks.* London: Longmans, Green, Longmans, and Roberts, 1860.

Shapiro, Eli. "Credit Controls and Financial Intermediaries," *Conference on Savings and Residential Financing, 1965 Proceedings.* Chicago: United States Savings and Loan League, 1961.

Shaw, Edward S. *Savings and Loan Structure and Market Performance.* Los Angeles: Savings and Loan Commissioner, State of California, 1962.

Shelby, Donald. "Some Implications of the Growth of Financial Intermediaries," *Journal of Finance,* Vol. XIII (December, 1958).

Sherman, Franklin J. *Modern Story of Mutual Savings Banks.* New York: Little and Ives, 1934.

Shull, Bernard, and Paul M. Horvitz. "Branch Banking and the Structure of Competition," *National Banking Review,* Vol. I, No. 3 (March, 1964).

Smelser, Neil J. *Social Change in the Industrial Revolution.* Chicago: University of Chicago Press, 1959.

Smith, Tynan. "Research on Banking Structure and Performance," *Federal Reserve Bulletin,* April, 1966.

Smith, Warren L. "Financial Intermediaries and Monetary Controls," *Quarterly Journal of Economics,* Vol. LXXIII (November, 1959).

Smith, William Paul. "Measures of Banking Structure and Competition," *Federal Reserve Bulletin,* September, 1965.

Solomon, Ezra. "Financial Institutions in the Savings-Investment Process," *Conference on Savings and Residential Financing, 1959 Proceedings.* Chicago: United States Savings and Loan League, 1959.

Steiner, W. H. *Mutual Savings Bank Liquidity: A Report to the Committee on Corporate Securities.* New York: National Association of Mutual Savings Banks, 1957.

—— "Mutual Savings Banks," *Law and Contemporary Problems.* Durham, N.C.: Duke University School of Law, Winter, 1952.

Stevens, Edward J. "Deposits at Savings and Loan Associations," *Yale Economic Essays,* Vol. VI (Fall, 1966).

Strunk, Norman. "Commercial Banks Come Alive," *Savings and Loan News,* September, 1965.

—— "A Federal System of Mutual Savings Banks?" *Savings and Loan News,* Vol. LXXXVI, No. 5 (May, 1963).

—— "A New Era in Savings and Loan Business," *Savings and Loan Annals,* 1962.

T. K. Sanderson Organization. *Directory of American Savings and Loan Associations.* Baltimore: T. K. Sanderson Organization, 1965–66.

Theobald, A. D. *Partners in Progress*. Address at the 16th Midyear Meeting of the National Association of Mutual Savings Banks, December 2, 1962.

Tobin, James. "Commercial Banks as Creators of 'Money'?" in Deane Carson, ed., *Banking and Monetary Studies*. Homewood, Ill.: Richard D. Irwin, 1963.

—— "Money, Capital and Other Stores of Value," *American Economic Review, Papers and Proceedings*, Vol. XV (May, 1961).

Tobin, James, and William C. Brainard. "Financial Intermediaries and the Effectiveness of Monetary Controls," *American Economic Review, Papers and Proceedings*, Vol. LIII (May, 1963).

Torgerson, Harold W. "Developments in Savings and Loan Associations, 1945 to 1953," *Journal of Finance*, Vol. IX (September, 1954).

Torrance, Charles M. "Gross Flows of Funds Through Savings and Loan Associations," *Journal of Finance*, Vol. XV (May, 1960).

United States Building and Loan League. *Building and Loan Annals*. Chicago: United States Building and Loan League, 1930–38.

United States Savings and Loan League. *Savings and Loan Annals*. Chicago: United States Savings and Loan League, 1939–64.

—— *Savings and Loan Fact Book*. Chicago: United States Savings and Loan League, 1964–65.

Welfling, Weldon. *Savings Banking in New York State*. Durham, N.C.: Duke University Press, 1939.

Werboff, Lawrence L., Marvin E. Rozen, *et al.* "Market Shares and Competition among Financial Institutions," in Commission on Money and Credit, *Private Financial Institutions*. Englewood Cliffs, N.J.: Prentice-Hall, 1963.

Willis, J. Brooke. "Gross Flows of Funds Through Mutual Savings Banks," *Journal of Finance*, Vol. XV (May, 1960).

Wolff, Henry W. *Peoples Banks*. London: P. S. King, 1919.

Wrigley, Edmund. *How to Manage Building Associations*. Philadelphia: J. K. Simon, 1880.

UNPUBLISHED MATERIAL

Blankenship, Ostberg, Inc. "Attitudes of New York State Residents Towards Savings Banks." New York: Blankenship, Ostberg, Inc., 1963.

Bodfish, Morton. "Depression Experience of Savings and Loan Associations in the United States." Address delivered in Salzburg, Austria, before the Fifth International Congress of Building and Loan Associations, September, 1935. Chicago: United States Savings and Loan League, 1935.

Fredrickson, E. Bruce. "The Federal Home Loan Bank System: Some Aspects of Savings Bank Membership." Research Department, National Association of Mutual Savings Banks, November, 1961.

Murray, Roger F. "Mutual Funds as a Service for Savings Banks." New York: Savings Banks Association of the State of New York, 1960. (Mimeographed.)

—— "Savings Bank Investment Policy over the Business Cycle." Address before the 13th Annual Midyear Meeting of the National Association of Mutual Savings Banks, New York, December 8, 1959. (Mimeographed.)

Redfield, John J. "Savings Banks and Savings and Loan Associations, the Past and the Future." Address before the Committee on Savings and Loan Associations of the Banking and Business Law Section of the American Bar Association, Washington, D.C., August 27, 1960. (Mimeographed.)

Root, Oren. "Statement before the Joint Legislative Committee to Revise the Banking Law." New York: New York Banking Department, released January 30, 1963.

Savings Banks Association of New York State. "Locations of Main Offices and Branches of Commercial Banks, Savings Banks, and Savings and Loan Associations in New York State, 1963." New York: Savings Banks Association of New York State, 1963. (Mimeographed.)

Stanford Research Institute. "California Savings and Loan Associations." Pasadena, Calif.: Stanford Research Institute, 1959. (Mimeographed.)

Walker, Charles E. "The Dual Banking System—Its Strengths and Weaknesses." Address before the annual convention of the Financial Public Relations Association, Atlantic City, N.J., October 15, 1962.

PUBLIC DOCUMENTS

Committee on Financial Institutions. *Report of the Committee on Financial Institutions to the President of the United States.* Washington, D.C.: Government Printing Office, 1963.

Economic Report of the President and Annual Report of the Council of Economic Advisors. Washington, D.C.: Government Printing Office, 1967.

New York State Banking Department. *Branch Banking, Bank Mergers and the Public Interest.* New York: New York State Banking Department, 1964.

—— *Postwar Banking Developments in New York State.* New York: New York State Banking Department, 1958.

—— *Report of the Superintendent of Banks, State of New York.* New York: New York State Banking Department, 1945–64.

U.S. Bureau of Labor. *Ninth Annual Report, Commissioner of Labor.* Washington, D.C.: Government Printing Office, 1894.

U.S. Bureau of the Census. *United States Census of Population, United States Summary.* 1950–60. Washington, D.C.: Government Printing Office, 1951–61.

—— *United States Census of Population and Housing, 1960, Final Report.* Vol. 104, Pt. 1. Washington, D.C.: Government Printing Office, 1962.

U.S. Congress. *Home Owner's Loan Act of 1933.* 73rd Congress, 1st Session, 1933.

U.S. House of Representatives. Committee on Banking and Currency. *Comparative Regulations of Financial Institutions.* 88th Congress, 1st Session, 1963.

—— *Federal Charter Legislation for Mutual Savings Banks, H. R. 258.* 88th Congress, 1st Session, 1963.

—— *Hearings on H.R. 258, Federal Charter Legislation for Mutual Savings Banks.* 88th Congress, 1st Session, 1963.

—— Committee on Ways and Means. *Revenue Act of 1962.* House Report No. 1447. 87th Congress, 2d Session, 1962.

Index